DECORATING

with

Southern Living®

DECORATING

with

Southern Living®

Louis Joyner

with the
Homes Staff of
SOUTHERN LIVING
Magazine

Carole Engle
Ernest Wood
Linda Hallam
Deborah Hastings
John O'Hagan
Cheryl Sales

Oxmoor
House®

Library of Congress Catalog Number: 88-64043
ISBN: 0-8487-0772-9
Manufactured in the United States of America

First Edition

Executive Editor: Nancy J. Fitzpatrick
Production Manager: Jerry Higdon
Associate Production Manager: Rick Litton
Art Director: Bob Nance

Decorating with SOUTHERN LIVING

Editor: Rebecca Brennan
Designer: Earl Freedle
Editorial Assistant: Karolyn Morgan
Production Assistant: Theresa L. Beste

Frontis: John O'Hagan

To subscribe to *Southern Living*® magazine, write
to *Southern Living,* P.O. Box C-119, Birmingham, AL 35283

CONTENTS

INTRODUCTION

*I*n decorating your own home, you face many choices. Almost too many, in fact. Decorating your own home can be one of the most challenging—and traumatic—of experiences. It's tempting just to turn the whole job over to a designer, give him a blank check, and go on vacation for a few months. But most of us can't do it that way. We have to nibble away at the house a room at a time. Or even a corner at a time. That means that we are never really finished decorating our homes, but then they're never boring, either.

When you do the decorating yourself, you have the flexibility to change your home as your family's needs change. You can adjust your home and its furnishings to meet your own changing sense of style. You can really make it yours.

Developing your own sense of style, however, takes time and effort. Even if you are working with a design professional, it helps to have an understanding of the design process and of home furnishings. That's where this book comes in.

Decorating with Southern Living is organized on a room-by-room basis, because that's the way most of us decorate. Obviously, there's a lot of carryover among the chapters. For example, information on color appears in chapter three, but the use of color, whether paint or fabric, is not limited to the living room. Even if you are working only on a single room, take the time to browse through the entire book. You may find that one of the built-in bookcases pictured in the chapter on family rooms would be perfect for your master bedroom. Or the mirrored wall that visually enlarges an entry in chapter two could do the same thing in a crowded bath.

The index will be a big help to you in finding specific information within the book. Highlighted tips boxes scattered throughout the text give you information on the more technical aspects of home decorating, as well as concise information on decorating specifics. The glossary at the end of the book will explain some of the terms used in the design profession. Somehow, the word *aubergine* isn't quite so off-putting when you realize it's simply a French word for an eggplant color.

If your decorating budget is small, a design professional can be a great help in mapping out a long-range plan for your home. It may take five years or forever, but you will have a goal, and you won't be buying pieces haphazardly. Purchases can be planned for both an immediate need and a long-term goal. For example, inexpensive director's chairs could serve as living room seating for a first apartment, then be used for casual dining chairs in a first house. Later, they could provide extra seating in a basement playroom. The important thing to remember is to buy well-designed furnishings that will last and not go out of style. Likewise, choosing basic fabrics and wall colors that will not seem dated in a year or two will help you avoid the extra cost and trouble of redoing the interior too often.

Learning about design and home furnishings isn't necessarily easy, but it can be—and should be—fun. Studying about new things, or old ones such as antiques, is a good way to begin to understand your own preferences. Read, look, ask questions. You don't need to know everything about all phases of interior design, but you'll be amazed at how much specific information you can pick up in a relatively short time.

At the same time, you'll be learning a bit of history—about how our ancestors lived, what their homes were like, and why. You'll develop a better understanding of historic homes and a better appreciation of the craftsmanship and artistry of the early furniture makers.

Remember that decorating your home should be a personal experience, even if you use the help of a design professional. Your home should express your interests and personality, as well as those of your family. An antique brought back from a vacation or an heirloom passed down from your ancestors will have much more meaning to you, and to your guests, than a piece simply selected to fill an empty spot. It is these personal touches that bring a feeling of warmth and creativity to your home.

$\mathcal{W}$here to put the lamp? Which color for the wall? A print or solid fabric for the sofa? Decorating demands decisions. The first consideration, and the most important one, is choosing a style that expresses your own personality.

A STYLE FOR YOU

ACHIEVING YOUR STYLE

Rich and warm, distinctive colors and military accessories bring a decidedly masculine look to this retreat. Gold epaulets flank the portrait above the mantel; the wall covering is a moiré fabric. Often an entire decorating scheme for a room can be shaped around personal collections and mementos.

When selecting a decorating look for your home, remember that there is no right or wrong style. Certainly, some styles are more popular than others, and that popularity changes over time. But the basics of good design—pleasing proportions, harmonious colors, and appropriate scale—remain constant.

The look you want to achieve for your home is your starting place. Consider many different styles before you decide on the one best suited to your personality and lifestyle. Study the photographs in this chapter and throughout the book. Consult other books and magazines. Visit showhouses. Soon certain characteristics will emerge from those rooms you favor. Analyze why you like each room. Is it the color scheme? The individual pieces of furniture? The fabrics? The accessories? Do you like the layered, somewhat fussy look of English Country? Or do you prefer sleek, stark Contemporary? Do you like antiques and

collectibles? Keep in mind that, after all, it is your home, and you should decorate it for you and your family. You should feel comfortable with your decorating style; then your guests will feel at ease, too.

Decorating is a process, not a product. Creating an attractive, functional home interior requires effort and insight, as well as artistic ability and technical knowledge. To help with the process, it is a good idea to call upon a trained professional, an interior designer who can work with you to achieve the look you want.

Working in collaboration with a designer offers a number of advantages: professional designers have many resources readily available, including showrooms that are open only to members of the design professions; they have years of experience designing home interiors; many make frequent buying trips, both to domestic furniture and accessories markets, as well as overseas markets; and, most importantly, a trained designer can actually save you money by helping you avoid costly mistakes.

The time to consult a designer is during the initial planning stages, whether you are building new or remodeling. At this point, changes can be made easily—and often in the case of new construction, with minimal cost. Making changes after construction has been completed can be expensive.

Finding the right designer is simply a matter of choosing a designer whose work appeals to you. Reputable designers usually have color photographs of their work, and sometimes you can see their work at actual sites by appointment.

Designers who have had at least six years of formal schooling and field experience and have proven their skills in both written and practical tests are allowed to use the initials ASID (American Society of Interior Designers) after their names. Membership does not necessarily guarantee quality and competence, but it is

another checkpoint in obtaining professional guidance. Many excellent designers are not ASID, either by choice or because they have had too little experience to qualify. By writing to the American Society of Interior Designers, 1430 Broadway, New York, New York 10018, you can locate an ASID member near you.

Part of the candid relationship between designer and client involves money matters. You should have some idea of how much you want to spend and how much you are willing to budget for later before talking with your designer. Ask right away how your designer charges. Most designers charge in one of three basic ways: a set fee, an hourly rate, or a percentage of sales.

Designers seldom charge a set fee unless they know the amount of time the job will take and what services they will be providing. A master plan usually falls into this category. A master plan typically includes a floor plan, perspective sketches, and a list of selections, including samples of fabric, wallpaper, paint, and flooring. The master plan approach appeals to many people because they know in advance what the design service will cost; they have a professional look they could not have achieved on their own; and they can wait and, perhaps, buy some items on sale.

Most interior designers charge by the hour for time spent consulting, making purchases, and supervising the installation of a design. Generally, fees range from

thirty dollars to one hundred dollars per hour. Designers may charge for traveling time and expenses, as well. Some have a minimum hourly fee and a higher price for an initial visit. Often, furniture stores and design firms will provide a designer's services at no charge if you purchase from them.

Many independent designers choose to work for a percentage of sales instead of charging a design fee. This percentage is actually a discount the merchant gives the designer for doing business with him. In effect, the client gets quality furnishings plus the designer's expertise for the price of the furnishings only.

A designer may use a combination of billing practices. For instance, if you go with your designer to the wholesale furnishing market, the charge for design services may switch from an hourly fee to a percentage of the purchases.

Drawing up a contract during the initial stages of design is usually a good idea; then there are no misunderstandings about what the designer is expected to handle. Remember, however, that there are some aspects of interior designing that go beyond the control of the designer. Deliveries can be late or factories can be out of certain fabrics or furniture. But you can expect the design professional to keep you informed on the status of all orders and respond to your inquiries as quickly as possible.

Eighteenth-Century English

A high point of furniture production in England, the eighteenth century became known for its Queen Anne and Chippendale styles. The first derived its name from the reigning monarch and the latter from Thomas Chippendale, whose excellent furniture designs are still being copied today.

Eighteenth-century English is a refined style and can be either very formal in feeling or slightly more relaxed, depending on the upholstered pieces. The primary wood used in this style is mahogany, often accented with banding or inlaid designs or cut to expose beautiful graining patterns. The dark wood tones enhance this style's dressy look.

Characteristic fabrics for this look are the more formal ones such as silk or damask. The fabric colors can be soft or vibrant but often have a grayed tone to them, as do the wall colors. In upholstered pieces, wing chairs and camelback sofas are primary components.

The Chippendale-style chairs, Oriental rug, and ornate mirror give this dining room a refined, dressy look. The walls are covered in a floral-and-vine motif paper with a paneled wainscot below.

❖ To establish your decorating scheme, shop in a store that specializes in eighteenth-century reproductions. There is usually an in-store designer who can help you with your selections.

❖ Antiques are suitable with most styles, but they are particularly appropriate with this one. Again, a reputable dealer can help you choose pieces that are in keeping with the look you want to achieve.

❖ Large lap trays with straight-legged stands work well as small chair-side tables.

❖ Lamps appropriate to this look can be in a variety of materials, including porcelain, brass, and crystal, but in traditional styling.

❖ Ornate mirrors are used in foyers, over sideboards, above chests. They can be Queen Anne or Chippendale in style. Oriental-style mirrors add an intriguing complement, as well.

❖ All varieties of Oriental rugs can be used successfully with the Eighteenth-century English look.

❖ Accessories, especially crystal and brass, add touches of sparkle to any decorating scheme. Traditionally styled candlesticks covered with glass lanterns provide a simple, elegant way to accessorize tables, mantels, and chests.

❖ Small wooden boxes, delicate silver objects, and pewter pieces also enhance this particular style.

English Country

For centuries, the English have retreated to their country homes for rest, relaxation, and the enjoyment of life's simple pleasures. Often, the country houses have been in their families for generations, acquiring a well-lived-in aura of comfort and ease. The English Country look is more an ambience than a distinct combination of elements. With this style, we have come to associate an atmosphere highlighted by comfortable furnishings, roaring fires, billowy curtains, and soft, cotton slipcovers.

Leading the list of fabrics for an English Country look are big-patterned chintzes, florals to bring the garden indoors, and Chinese motifs to echo a fondness for Oriental themes. Many of the typical colors used to evoke an English Country setting derive from Oriental rug colors—the roses, burgundies, and medium to navy blues.

Upholstery pieces not only look inviting, but are plushy with down or other soft filling. Rolled arms, throw pillows, and overstuffed backs add to the "come sit down" look. Accessories are added as accent pieces, but many also serve as amenities to relaxing, such as lap throws, footstools, and small benches.

Piled high with plush pillows, this small sofa creates an inviting sitting area. The English Country aura of this bedroom comes from the cozy, comfortable blending of rose-colored fabrics, soft pillows, and an atmosphere of blissful relaxation.

Comfortable, yet elegant, this room combines several elements for distinctive English Country style: floral upholstery fabrics accented with fringe, footstools used as accessories and amenities to relaxing, and prominently displayed collectibles. The swagged window treatment is set inside the frame, allowing the painted molding to show.

❖ Books are a fitting accent in the English Country room. Display them on coffee tables, occasional tables, secretaries; stack them, perhaps leave some open, ready to enjoy.

❖ Wall brackets, botanical prints, mirrors, oil paintings of still lifes or pastoral landscapes add a full, rich look to the walls.

❖ Needlepoint accents offer the charm of a handmade look. Many copies of old Victorian designs are available.

❖ Display collections prominently. Staffordshire, blue and white, statuary, even vases or bowls filled with handfuls of fresh flowers or herbs add a pleasing familiarity to the room.

❖ The warm tones of brass accessories highlight the soft appeal of this comfortable style.

❖ Cotton slipcovers trimmed with fringe or a contrasting color offer a fresh, casual look, especially appropriate in summer.

The low, beamed ceiling, dark paneling, and exposed log wall help turn back the clock in this restored dogtrot cabin. Simple cotton curtains allow optimum light to shine through the small windows. The American Country decor has a more rustic look than the Colonial style.

The Colonial period of American art and architecture extended from the 1600s up to the Revolution. It was a time when the blending of different cultures, namely English, French, and Dutch, created a style influenced by elements from each. The style that evolved has a more pro-vincial look than either Eigh-teenth-century English or Formal French. As with English Country or Country French, furniture pieces are chunky and rustic looking. Walnut and oak are the favored woods, imparting a warm look to interiors.

Colors commonly used with an American Colonial look are medium to navy blues mixed with rusty reds. Plaids and checks in these color combinations are fre-quently seen on upholstered pieces, as are textured linens or cottons. Wall colors vary, but a warm, rusty red is often used for family rooms and, oc-casionally, for kitchens.

American Country is closely related to this style, only more rusticated. Accesso-ries and furniture pieces are more primitive, many with the original paint left in its unre-touched condition. Usually rooms are minimally furnished with basic, functional furniture pieces only. Simple arrange-ments of wildflowers and fruit are especially fitting in this type setting.

❖ Folk art accents enhance the American Colonial look.

❖ Use accessory pieces with a decidedly Colonial or folk art flavor, such as porcelain hens, ducks, and geese.

❖ Lamp bases can range from colorful tins to coarsely textured jugs.

❖ Pierced tin is a good choice for chandeliers; lanterns are also a good lighting accent for this style.

❖ Woven or rag rugs, often oval in shape, add color and texture to the decorating scheme and also help to harmonize colors. They are especially charming in an American Country scheme.

Boxed ceiling beams and raised paneling reinforce the Colonial feel of this family room. Carefully chosen accessories, such as the basket of pine cones, the handmade broom, and the ceramic chickens, further the effect. The flame-stitch fabric on the wing chair and the quilt draped over the Windsor chair are both in shades of rust and blue in keeping with the period.

Formal French

For a dressy look, consider a Formal French style. Period pieces, particularly chairs, chests, and consoles from the Louis XIV, XV, and XVI periods, add a touch of European ambience to any room setting. Most furniture of this look reveals an abundance of carving and painting, though it retains a delicate quality even when quite ornate.

Instead of dark wood tones, a Formal French look relies on fruitwoods, which are more suitable for the painting and gilding associated with this style. Often wood pieces have cream, white, or pastel finishes, frequently highlighted with gold. For this style, straight lines are replaced with graceful curves, such as on the bombé chest, and fluted legs take the place of plain ones.

This dressed-up sitting room features the graceful lines commonly associated with a Formal French decor. The marble mantelpiece is characterized by its delicate carving and detail, as well.

❖ Along with fruitwoods, other materials associated with a Formal French look are marble and ornate ironwork; marble is used often atop chests, ornate ironwork on consoles.

❖ Chests and tables frequently exhibit intricate marquetry, small contrasting wood inlays forming elaborate patterns, especially diamond patterns.

❖ Silk and brocade fabrics typify the Formal French look; many fabrics employ tiny gold threads as part of a floral design.

Soft colors and a subtle mix of solid and floral fabrics lend a distinctive French look to this living room. The large paneled area above the mantel is pickled to echo the light finish of the Louis XV chair.

Country French

The Country French style is similar to the English Country look in that it is a celebration of a simpler life-style, a relaxed way of doing things. It is a heavier, more countrified version of the rococo style, an Early American look with a French accent. Furniture is usually walnut, oak, or fruitwood, with simple lines and less veneer, marquetry, and ornate carving.

Cotton is the primary fabric used in establishing a Country French look, especially cottons with small, repetitive prints such as tiny stylized flowers, fleurs-de-lis, or miniature geometrics. Often these patterns are combined with tiny stripes. The backgrounds for these fabrics are not pure white, but oatmeal, cream, or banana colors.

Window treatments are simple, often swags used in conjunction with plain, lace curtains.

❖ Use needlepoint rugs or area rugs with flower-and-vine patterns.

❖ Choose small dining chairs with simple carving or crosspieces; cushion with ruffled pillows.

❖ Use pull-up chairs with rush or cane seats.

❖ A large French armoire with simple carving provides handy storage for electronic equipment or linens, while reinforcing the decorating scheme.

❖ Mix fruitwoods, such as pecan or apple, with oak or walnut pieces.

❖ Display decorative plates on walls. Hang them in a row, frame a door, or form a circle around a bracket holding a plant.

❖ Small porcelains, particularly figurines, make colorful and interesting accent pieces.

An antique French cast-stone mantel adds a distinctive focal point to this garage converted to a casual living area. Concrete pavers, cast to match the colors of the mantel, form the chimney breast. The chairs and sofa are covered in blue-and-white pillow ticking. Decorative plates are used as accent pieces.

Southwest Flair

"Sparse and simple" describes the Southwest look. Borrowing heavily from American Indian and Mexican motifs, this decorating style pulls together the best elements from each to create a unique look, rather than a simple imitation of the original influences. While seen primarily in the West and Southwest, this decorating scheme is experiencing increasing popularity in other areas. It is a decor particularly suited to mountain and weekend retreats, since the colors and shapes of nature contribute substantially to its character.

The background for a Southwest look is more simple than that for other styles. For example, wall colors tend to be neutral—pale tans, creams, or even the palest peach or terra-cotta tones. Window treatments range from very simple to completely bare. Where shade and privacy are needed, wide-slatted shutters, left natural, work well and provide the clean, uncluttered lines consistent with the Southwest style.

Upholstered pieces generally have a contemporary look. Large, overstuffed sofas, big chairs, and oversize ottomans are covered in white or cream-colored fabrics, often with a nubby texture or pile. Accent colors can be bright, perhaps suggested by artwork. Rag rugs or heavy, white wool rugs with double-knotted fringe help organize seating areas.

Wood furniture is usually pine or light oak and is primitive in look and construction. The period most often associated with this furnishing style is referred to as Early Mission Spanish, characterized by heavy, functional pieces able to withstand a great deal of wear.

Art enhances the Southwest look, perhaps more than any other one accessory. Artwork can be in a variety of mediums, but watercolor is a favorite. Simple framing is in keeping with the overall decor.

The traditional Southwest ceiling of vigas and latias adds an authentic touch to this remodeled living room. The rounded corner fireplace heightens the effect.

❖ Pale buff or cream walls emphasize light and provide an effective neutral backdrop for furniture and artwork.

❖ Wood trim can be left natural with a protective varnish finish or stained blonde. A pickled finish is ideal for the Southwest style.

❖ Mexican or Saltillo tile floors contribute earthy color and texture, both important elements in a Southwest decorating scheme.

❖ For an area rug, use a multicolored rag rug; these can be found in a wide variety of sizes.

❖ Native objects such as horns can be used for chandeliers, coffee table bases, or as objets d'art.

❖ Other materials used with this style are cast stone, especially for tables and table bases, and terra-cotta.

❖ Accessories can be primitive in appearance, supplying rich texture, shape, and color.

❖ Brightly striped throws or pillows in primary colors contribute a distinctive Mexican feeling.

❖ Use native plants sparingly—one small cactus plant is plenty.

Eclectic

For those who love a wide variety of decorating styles, Eclectic may be the best look; however, it is also one of the most difficult to do well because a mix of periods can result in a hodgepodge. The key to making the Eclectic style work is a well-defined color scheme. Color will pull together the various periods and help provide definition for different types of upholstery. For example, using the same fabric on chairs of the most divergent styles will create a unified, harmonious look.

Though the Eclectic look can accommodate a variety of styles, there are certain periods that do not mix well. For example, several pieces from different periods that are all very distinctive and ornate may not work together for a cohesive look. It is better to balance one ornate piece with one of simpler lines.

The Victorian period was actually considered a period of eclecticism since it borrowed older patterns and styles and adapted them to more modern uses.

Elegant Louis XV armchairs mix comfortably with an acrylic and marble cocktail table in this family room addition. In the foreground, a pair of Country French side chairs face a primitive pine farm table. The floor of the room is brick, the walls and ceiling are plywood siding wiped with white latex paint.

❖ A strong color scheme, well defined rather than subtle, works best for an Eclectic look.

❖ All kinds of artwork may be used, but they must be similarly framed to give a sense of unity.

❖ A variety of lamp styles can work for this look, but simple designs will not compete with other furnishings.

❖ If furniture pieces are ornate, use solid color fabrics. The solid colors will enhance the elaborate lines and details of the furniture.

❖ Choose accessories carefully to avoid a cluttered look.

❖ A touch of black added to the room setting helps ground the colors and styles—lampshades are a good place to do this.

For a sleek, Eclectic look, four black-lacquered Thonet chairs, circa 1910, cluster around a marble table. The chrome-and-glass chandelier is a contemporary Italian design.

Dark and rich, this Victorian parlor recalls the opulence of the late nineteenth century. Every available table surface is filled to overflowing with an eclectic mix of accessories.

The Victorian period in history covered the reign of Queen Victoria from 1837-1901. During that time, furniture makers became eclectic in the truest sense of the word, combining elements of many different styles, including Oriental, Italian Renaissance, and rococo. From the 1870s through the 1890s, the height of the period, furniture was massive and heavy in scale with extravagant use of moldings and classical motifs. Most pieces were overly embellished with curves, scrolls, and heavy carvings of birds, flowers, and fruits. Woods used were mainly rosewood, mahogany, and black walnut with marble used abundantly, especially on tabletops.

Along with large, ornate furnishings, the colors used with the Victorian look are deep and rich with a variety of patterns used one on top of another. Velvets and brocades are favorite fabrics, with lace doilies adorning not only upholstered pieces, but tables, chests, and sideboards as well.

Layer on layer, pattern on pattern, style on style—a Victorian decorating scheme requires an elaborate mix of patterns and colors to achieve its full effect.

Crisp, simple lines and a minimum of accessories give this living room a distinctive, Contemporary ambience. An ornate clock, displayed as a work of art, provides the focal point at the mantel.

A Contemporary decorating scheme usually calls to mind fine, clean lines, but the look can be stark and cold if not handled with skill. Because colors, upholstery pieces, and most furnishings are simple, this style calls for exciting, dramatic artwork and accents.

The Contemporary look uses neutrals accented with reds and blacks—the red often seen in artwork, the black in leather upholstery. Architectural furniture is a dominant feature, the pieces acting more like sculpture than furniture. In fact, many of these pieces were designed by well-known architects or designers and have reached the status of art objects themselves.

Leather is a common Contemporary-style upholstery fabric. It is durable and easy to care for, requiring only an occasional buffing with a leather moisture enhancer. With care it will last a lifetime, gaining a rich patina with age.

❖ Glass, chrome, or molded plastic accent pieces complement a Contemporary decorating scheme.

❖ Keep accessories to a minimum, allowing furnishings and wall art to be dominant.

❖ Large plants contribute interesting texture, shape, and warmth.

❖ Very little pattern is used for upholstered furnishings and on walls; large, bold blocks of color are formed by furniture, artwork, walls, and floors.

❖ Built-ins are a good way to maintain a clean, uncluttered look, while providing storage and display space.

❖ Large, sleek wall units with lots of glass are another storage option consistent with a Contemporary look.

❖ Laminated surfaces for tables and wall systems have a smooth, polished look and can be purchased in vibrant colors to accent a room's decor.

❖ Floor materials can range from wood to marble to ceramic tile.

❖ Commercial carpet with a tight pile is a good choice for floors and wears well.

❖ Lighting is crucial in any style, but especially for Contemporary decor. Choose track, recessed, or any of a variety of hanging fixtures. These, like certain furniture pieces, can add a sculptural aspect to the room design. Lighting creates mood and adds dramatic highlights.

Designed as a two-story atrium, this angled gallery displays a collection of twentieth-century glass and pottery. The glass block stairwall strengthens the sculptural quality of the space.

Lightened Looks

Regardless of the style you choose, the interpretation does not have to be a strict period representation. Lighter, fresher looks can be achieved by adding a few transitional or contemporary pieces. For example, in a traditional living room, a pair of armless chairs will lighten the look of heavier upholstered pieces such as wing chairs and large sofas. The same is true of a glass-topped coffee table, which can contribute interest with any of a variety of different bases. A piece of glass furniture mixed in with antiques and other traditional furnishings adds a bit of airiness to interiors.

Colors can play a significant role in creating a fresh interior. Pastel fabrics, available in a variety of patterns, can balance and highlight darker wood tones. Though there are exceptions, a good general rule to follow is if you plan to use strong patterns in the room for upholstery pieces, consider a wall color that is light to medium, rather than a vibrant, strong color that may compete with the fabrics. If, on the other hand, you plan to have several solid fabrics, particularly if the solids are also neutral in value, you may want to consider a more intense, dramatic wall color.

Touches of the past—moldings and a beaded ceiling—are lightened and freshened with soft shades of cream. Large windows, purposely left bare, add to the open, airy appeal of this new house.

A skirted table and windows left bare give a light, fresh look to this restored century-old house. Crisp white paint emphasizes the ornate trim and the room's twelve-foot-high ceiling.

❖ Glass table tops and glass accessories such as vases, lamps, and bowls create a look of spaciousness.

❖ Contemporary artwork, whether paintings, prints, or pottery, mixed with traditional furnishings lightens interiors.

❖ A glossy lampshade imparts a light, Contemporary appearance.

❖ For a lightened look, use a print or pattern that has pure white as a background, rather than cream or off-white.

❖ Any stripe will help add a fresh look, but one mixed with white adds an extra crispness.

❖ Mirroring a wall adds light and creates a sense of depth.

❖ Any of the newer looks in rugs, such as Berber or a dhurrie, gives a fresh accent.

FIRST IMPRESSIONS

own the walk,

up the steps to the front door . . .

a knock . . . your guests have arrived.

But before you welcome them, your

home does. Details show them the way,

comfortably and safely, to your door,

while expressing the quality and style

within. Through the door, the foyer

offers the first glimpse of your home's

style and personality.

THE FRONT DOOR

Front entries affect first impressions. Because the front entry is most often in a prominent location, a few well-chosen accents add welcoming touches to the overall appearance of the house.

Paint, hardware, and accessories can make a front door more inviting, but it is important also to consider the area surrounding the door. Plants in containers can be used to pull the landscaping up to the door, and a piece of furniture can carry the interior of the house outside.

A new front door can enhance the entire front of your house. If your door is a standard size, replacing it can be a relatively simple operation yielding impressive results. You will need to work with only a building supply company and a carpenter. If your door is an unusual size, or if you want a custom design or an antique door, you will have more details to consider.

Victorian gingerbread and cast-iron railings frame the shuttered front door of this quaint home.

❖ An antique door may be difficult to fit to your house, because antique doors often are non-standard sizes.

❖ If you have to trim an antique door to fit, do not trim off so much that you weaken the door. Also, be careful not to change the proportions to the extent that you alter the door's original design.

❖ Antique doors often come without hardware. If possible, select a door with holes that will accommodate modern knobs and locks or with holes that can be filled without showing.

❖ If the door was painted with a lead-base paint, you may not be able to remove all of the color before staining the door. The remaining "ghost" color will affect the color of the stain on the door.

❖ A painted door may have knots or other imperfections, and its grain may not be as beautiful as the grain in a door originally intended for staining.

❖ A custom door can cost two or three times as much as a stock door. A very elaborate door may cost even more.

❖ Many people who go to the trouble and expense of a custom door want a one-of-a-kind item. A millwork shop can make a door from an architect's or designer's plans or may be able to design the door from your own specifications. The millwork shop can recommend a local hardware supplier and will install the hardware on the door.

❖ A millwork company also can produce custom storm or screen doors, but many people choose to leave these off traditionally styled front doors.

❖ The style of the house will determine whether a door is painted or stained. The door on a Williamsburg-style house should be painted, for example. On a craftsman-style house, it should be stained.

❖ A rich accent color is the most dramatic and least expensive way to decorate the front door. When using a dramatic accent color such as red, paint only the front door that color. This calls attention to that door. The other doors should be painted the trim color.

❖ A stained door can be very attractive, but the door should be in a covered entry. Stained finishes do not hold up well when they are exposed to weather.

❖ Several coats of high-gloss varnish will protect any finish and enrich the accent color or stain. Use a marine varnish with an ultraviolet light absorber to prevent color fading and blistering.

A bright coat of red paint brings this row house door to life. Working shutters on the window enhance the authentic look, while brass accents complete the sleek impression.

The rich gleam of brass hardware on a door is evident even from the street. Brass, the most common material used for exterior hardware, tarnishes but does not rust as do most other metals. Much of the brass hardware sold today has a protective coating, so it will not require polishing. This finish will wear off in time, but kits are available to recoat the brass, or it can be left to oxidize naturally.

Special caution should be taken when installing brass hardware on metal, insulated doors. Kickplates and name plaques will need a cork backing, and brass sheet metal screws, which are not always included with the hardware, must be used.

Accessories

Brass accessories—kickplates, mail slot, knocker, and doorknob and plate—add sparkle to this otherwise dark double-entry door. Lush ferns soften the entrance.

Plants

Accent plants at the front door can be in containers or actually planted around the entry, such as a vine growing over a doorway. The size, shape, and texture of a planter can add special interest to the entry. Potted plants must be carefully monitored to make sure that they have enough water; soil in planters dries out quickly, especially in bright sunlight. Plants in containers probably will need to be watered every day.

Shrubs and flowering plants such as hibiscus are attractive in large planters. Evergreens pruned into topiary forms add year-round greenery to the entry. The direction the entry faces and the amount of shade it receives should be taken into consideration when choosing plants to grace your front door.

Vibrant flowers and lush greenery add welcoming appeal to this Charleston-style house.

Furniture

Furniture at the entry to your home should be distinctive. Even a simple bench should reflect the style of the house. Large pieces of furniture can be especially useful in balancing doorways that are positioned off-center.

Any furniture used outside must be able to take the weather. Ideally, painted pieces should be protected from the elements by a covering. Furniture that is uncovered should be designed to shed water.

Plenty of seating turns this large entrance porch into an outdoor living area. White paint unifies the mix of furniture styles.

Entry Lighting

A welcoming glow of light accents the details at the entry and brings your home to life at night. Lighting at the front door does double duty, for it is both decorative and functional. Properly designed illumination offers a warm greeting and keeps the entry safe and secure.

Usually, one fixture cannot light the entry adequately. Most entrances, especially those with porches or recessed front doors, need two types.

The most effective entryway lighting includes a decorative fixture beside the door and a downlight above. If the entrance is tall, the overhead light may be a lantern, globe, or other hanging fixture. In most cases, however, a recessed or surface-mounted downlight works best. The downlight not only lights the door, but creates a warmer welcome once the door is opened, because it lights the person in the doorway. From a distance, a recessed overhead light cannot be seen, giving the illusion that the decorative fixtures alone light the door.

Properly designed exterior lighting combined with the warm glow from the inside produces a dramatic, welcoming effect. A white fabric, gathered top and bottom on rods, ensures privacy.

❖ For soft lighting, use frosted rather than clear bulbs. To make the entire fixture appear to be the source of light, select one with frosted glass.

❖ A recessed light will attract fewer insects than exposed lights. Similarly, dimly lit decorative lanterns beside the door will not attract as many insects as bright ones.

❖ Mount wall lanterns sixty-six inches above the floor level at the door and install 25- to 60-watt frosted bulbs. Overhead lights should allow a seven-foot minimum clearance and be fitted with 60- to 100-watt frosted bulbs.

❖ Be careful not to overlight the door. The eyes of a person approaching the house will be adjusted to darkness, so a light that is too bright will be uncomfortable. It also can overpower the decorative effects of the fixture.

❖ Adjust the light level by changing the bulbs. Dimmer switches are another option, but it is more difficult to keep a constant lighting level with them.

❖ Let the overhead light illuminate the steps. Avoid lighting steps from the front. Lighting from above leaves the riser dark, making the steps easier to see.

❖ If your door has beveled or stained glass, install lights on the inside and direct them at the glass to show off patterns.

❖ Consider installing automatic timers to turn exterior lights on at dusk and off at dawn.

❖ If your home has a porch, you can light the door with spotlights placed under the eaves. If you do, be careful to adjust the lights so that they do not shine directly into the eyes of the person opening the door.

❖ Make sure that your lights are suitable for exterior installation. Exposed lights can collect water at certain angles, ultimately requiring rewiring or replacing if they were intended for interior use only.

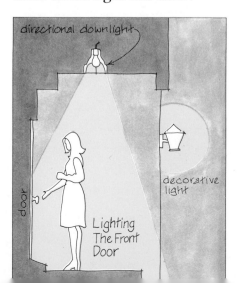

THE FOYER

Whether your foyer is a grand hall or a space just large enough to turn around in, it should make a dramatic statement. And, though your guests spend only a short time there, the foyer sets the tone for the rest of the house.

When planning your foyer, remember that it is your guests' first look at your house and that look should be impressive. So give it impact.

A few time-tested tips for creating a memorable foyer revolve around the idea of using one very striking technique to achieve the desired effect, such as upholstering walls; choosing an interesting paint finish, strié or marbleizing, for example; adding textures; using deep, rich colors; or even mirroring part or all of the foyer wall space. Using any one of these techniques creates a high-intensity look, especially for a small space.

Replacing a wall with arches and columns opened the living room to the foyer and created a strong visual impact upon entering the house. The black-and-white tile floor defines the entry.

Custom-designed white pine doors, surrounded by fixed sidelights and an arched transom, open to this airy foyer. Stained walnut insets are cut into the bleached oak floor. Ionic capitals top the round columns.

The bright floral wall covering chosen for this entry suggested fabric colors for the rest of the house. The floral paper has an open pattern that allows much of the creamy white background to show through.

❖ Since first impressions are so important, always use the highest quality accessories for your entry. For example, large Oriental-style area rugs can be rather costly, but a smaller, thus more affordable rug can contribute rich color and texture to a foyer floor.

❖ The same is true for chair upholstery fabrics. Choose a chair with only an upholstered seat or seat and back, and you can use an expensive fabric with little risk of wear and tear. A handsome shield-back chair or even a pretty settee covered with a silk or moiré fabric can be an interesting focal point in this setting, and a chair or bench is also a practical addition to the entryway furnishings.

❖ If your front door opens directly into the living room, use a screen or large piece of furniture to create the feeling of a foyer.

❖ Use a floor material that will set off the foyer from the rest of the house. A durable, long-wearing material, such as tile, can add a rich look to the area for a modest investment.

❖ Lighting should both illuminate the entry and accent special touches such as artwork or furniture. Use a dimmer switch to control the light level of the fixtures.

Extra foyer space can work double duty. Here, a bright corner is just the spot for a writing desk and pair of French-style chairs. Chintz drapery panels are shirred on a curtain rod, creating a luxurious effect.

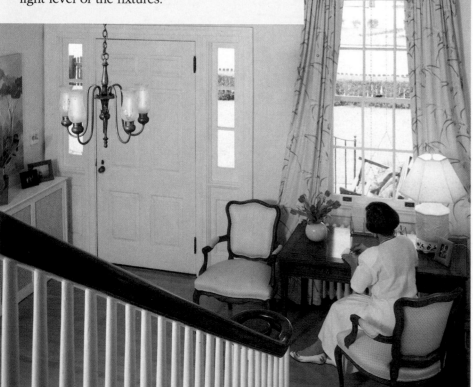

A large foyer can accommodate larger pieces of furniture, such as this handsome settee. The fine fabric and area rug add a touch of elegance. White painted surfaces and the Mexican tile floor mix with beveled and leaded glass to give this entryway an eclectic flair.

Walls

Walls can make an important decorating statement, especially in a small foyer area. Paint, deftly applied, can turn an ordinary entry into a work of art. When space is tight, what better way to open up a foyer than to fool the eye with a trompe l'oeil painting on the wall?

Another way to add drama to the entryway is to use a deep, rich wall color. Or you may choose to lighten a too-dark foyer with a light-colored paint or paper. Whichever you choose, it should contrast with the adjoining room for maximum impact.

Because dark paint colors were used in the adjoining room, lighter walls in the foyer give the space its own special look. A transom and side-lights allow natural sunlight to fill the area, while the hinged, louvered shutters control the amount of light.

Deft shading creates a niche in this painted entry wall.

A scenic French paper provides a fanciful accent to this small section of wall tucked under the stair. The wall below the chair rail is painted to repeat the foliage color of the scene.

Tables

A table can be a featured accent in a foyer. Tables offer a convenient place for mail and keys, as well.

In a narrow foyer, a slender console table is ideal. Some tables are available that are less than twelve inches wide. A wall-mounted shelf serves the same purpose and takes up very little space.

To add emphasis to the setting, hang a decorative mirror or painting above the table. For a bit of drama, create a simple still-life arrangement on the tabletop.

An Oriental-style console table, covered with grass cloth and painted a glossy black, stands in this entry. The tall basket fills the space below the table and repeats the warm colors of the Mexican tile floor.

Pine brackets, stripped of paint, support a beveled glass top. Architectural fragments, such as the brackets, are available from some wrecking companies or antique shops. The narrow shelf is well suited for a small entryway.

Stacked books, knotted fabric, a bowl of fruit, and other small objects create a serene still life atop this entryway table. A pair of tall lamps illuminate the arrangement.

Mirrors

A floor-to-ceiling mirror on one wall of this entry gives the area a more spacious appearance. The mirrored wall reflects the natural light from the door, creating an open, airy ambience. A gray faux-marble finish accents the baseboard.

Mirrors are a perfect solution for a too-small foyer. They visually expand the space and provide maximum light and reflection.

Choosing the right mirror for the setting is important. Consider the color of the frame and the colors in the room; cool colors work well with silver Venetian mirrors, while a gilded frame is very appealing with warm colors.

To achieve a dramatic effect, you may consider mirroring one or more walls. Usually, wall-mounted mirrors are attached in panels, above the baseboards. The mirror can be cut to size for outlets, if needed. Mirroring a wall is tricky and, in most cases, is a job for professionals. However, mirror tiles can be purchased for relatively simple do-it-yourself installation.

As an alternative to mirroring an entire wall, try hanging a new or antique wall mirror in the foyer. Although there are no hard-and-fast rules, keep in mind the size of the room, the dimensions of the wall, and the piece of furniture over which the mirror will hang. If possible, hang the mirror near a window so that it can reflect the light.

A wall-mounted mirror, framed to look like a window, fills the blank wall at this stair landing. Brass rods hold the stair runner in place. The simple balustrade is a variation of a Chippendale design.

❖ To hang a mirror: Use a heavy-duty picture hook—two or more if the mirror is large and heavy. If possible, nail or screw the hanger through the wall into a wall stud for extra support. If this is not possible, you can use a picture hook attached to a toggle bolt that goes through the gypsum wallboard. Hang the mirror at a comfortable viewing height. For the most pleasing proportions when hanging a large mirror over a chest or similar piece of furniture, position the bottom of the mirror four to six inches from the top of the chest.

An ornately carved pine frame in a natural wood finish adds distinction to this mirror. The size was chosen to fit within the wall panel. The placement of the mirror enables it to capture the illumination from the front door's fanlight.

Stairs

Stairs bring a gracious and grand feeling to an entry. They lead the eye up and enrich the foyer with the details of railing and balusters. The stairway is the connection between floors, both physically and stylistically, so wall and trim colors should be the same for the entry and the stairwell.

Safety is a prime consideration on the staircase. Proper lighting and handrail placement should be incorporated into the design.

Elegantly simple, this gracefully curving stair forms an almost sculptural focal point for the entry. Diamonds of walnut add a rich accent to the natural finish oak floor.

❖ The stair lights should be switched at both the top and bottom of the staircase.

❖ Carpet runners should be tacked in place or held with decorative carpet rods.

❖ Most building codes require a handrail on one side of the stairway for stairs less than forty-four inches wide and a handrail on both sides for stairs wider than forty-four

inches. The handrail should be located between thirty and thirty-four inches above the leading edge of the tread.

❖ Balustrades should be designed so that a six-inch-diameter ball cannot pass between the balusters.

A low, glass-block wall and a simple steel-pipe handrail are the distinctive elements comprising this contemporary stairway.

The formal living room will never go out of style in the South. Whether our houses are small cottages or grand estates, we all like a place to entertain—and live—graciously. A handsome living room with comfortable seating and attractive accessories provides a warm welcome for guests as well as a quiet spot for private contemplation.

ROOMS FOR COMPANY

LIVING ROOMS

To relax the formality of the room, the two wing chairs and the sofa were covered with white slipcovers. A pair of pickled pine armchairs with flame-stitch fabric cushions also serve to lighten the look.

Today, it is easier than ever before to design a pretty and livable formal space. A wide range of new and classic fabrics and paint colors, along with the ready availability of antiques, quality reproductions, and fine custom pieces, make decorating fun.

Even in living rooms that tend toward the grand and sumptuous, decorating rules are relaxed and anything but rigid. Part of this attitude stems from the trend toward English Country and Eclectic looks which blithely mix styles, periods, and patterns.

We no longer create our prettiest, most formal rooms as set pieces. From the English, we have borrowed the time-honored concept of layering our furnishings. We are free to mix inherited pieces with auction finds, contemporary art with our favorite collectibles, creating a look that is simultaneously beautiful and a personal statement of style.

Classic good looks never go out of style. In this formal living room, two love seats covered in a moiré sheen are part of a symmetrical fireplace arrangement with antique tables and lamps. Daffodil yellow walls emphasize the intricate wall and ceiling molding.

(Overleaf) Yellow walls and a white sofa provide the background for this cheerful mix of plaid, print, and floral fabrics. Prints mix easily with plaid when the compatible colors share the same values.

Traditional furnishings, such as this camelback sofa and the Chippendale-style armchairs, gain extra impact from a more contemporary setting. The rich Oriental rug over the darkly stained oak floor helps to define the seating area.

Matching sofas anchor the two separate seating areas in this rectangular living room. The Coromandel screen, porcelains, and long altar table add the Oriental touches often found in English and American Colonial interiors.

Fireplaces

A fireplace creates a natural focal point in a room. Though the fireplace may be used only a few months of the year, the chimney breast above offers year-round decorating possibilities. Whichever style or decorating scheme you plan, always begin any fireplace work with safety in mind.

A grandly carved mantelpiece provides the focus for this richly elegant room. The brass fire screen fills the firebox when it is not in use.

❖ If you are adding or redoing a fireplace, make sure that the design you choose meets your local building code. Typical code requirements for masonry fireplaces do not allow combustible materials (including wood) within six inches of the fireplace opening.

❖ Make sure that combustible materials within twelve inches of the fireplace opening do not project out from the face of the surround more than ⅛ inch for every inch from the opening.

❖ Choose materials such as masonry or natural stone for the fireplace surround. Fired tiles, either painted or unpainted, or mirrored tiles are also acceptable; however, cultured marble, a synthetic material, can be combustible in some cases.

A tall space calls for a large piece of art. Here a contemporary print contrasts harmoniously with the traditional, carved mantel. Recessed lights highlight the fireplace area.

If you are designing a fireplace, remember that the mantel will set the tone for the room. Both antique and reproduction mantels are available in a wide range of styles, sizes, and materials, including carved wood and cast stone. Architects and interior designers often will custom design mantels, sometimes using stock moldings. Although there are no precise rules, it is important that the mantel match the scale and the architecture of the room.

To update a rustic living or family room, add a mantel shelf with brackets to a plain fireplace wall. Or replace a heavy, rustic shelf with a more refined one, perhaps edged with molding. Choose the size of the mantel in proportion to the height and width of the wall and make sure that the mantel hangs below eye level.

Painting an exposed brick fireplace wall gives a dramatic new look. Proper preparation includes brushing off dust and loose dirt and scrubbing the bricks with a brush dipped in a sudsy solution. If salt particles have accumulated, wash the bricks with a five-percent solution of muriatic acid and rinse. Allow the bricks to dry, then apply at least two coats of a masonry or latex interior paint to the surface.

Marbleizing adds architectural interest to the pilasters and capitals that flank this fireplace.

Supported by carved brackets, this mantel dresses up a formerly plain fireplace wall for a more refined look. A grouping of prints balances the height of the large, brick chimneypiece.

❖ Instead of a mirror or painting hung on the chimneypiece, mirror the chimney breast instead. For extra sparkle, hang a mirror on the mirrored chimneypiece.

❖ Hang a tapestry, an unframed canvas, or a hand-painted floorcloth above the mantel for casual elegance.

❖ Paint a faux finish, such as marble, on your plain wood mantel.

❖ Add stock molding to enhance and visually strengthen a simple, shelf-style mantel. Or use molding strips to give a plain chimneypiece the look of raised paneling. Decorative medallions applied to a plain mantel will contribute interesting detail, as well.

❖ Install a small recessed spotlight in the ceiling above the fireplace. Tall, slender candlestick lamps or a gallery light above artwork also offer interesting lighting possibilities. Or use wall-mounted swing-arm lamps or electric sconces to frame the fireplace with light.

❖ Enrich the firebox with accessories. New, reproduction, or antique fenders, andirons, tools, screens, and brass buckets add a decorative touch to this utilitarian space.

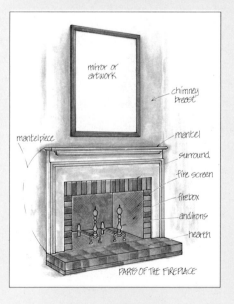

mirror or artwork

chimney breast

mantelpiece

mantel

surround

fire screen

firebox

andirons

hearth

PARTS OF THE FIREPLACE

63

Mantel Accessories

Tall, slender bookcases on either side of the fireplace give vertical emphasis to this small room. The walls are a dramatic medium dark gray-brown. Creamy white bookcases and trim make the wall color seem even more intense. The mantel has a gray, brown, and tan marbleized faux finish. Strewn across the mantel is a variety of unexpected items which accentuate the room's eclectic styling.

Safe, protected, and elevated, the mantel provides ideal display space. Small collections in particular, which may get lost when scattered about a room, gain impact when grouped together. To give a collection its most dramatic presentation, center a large painting, mirror, or wall hanging on the wall behind the arrangement. Or elevate small objects, such as porcelains, atop antique books for interesting height variation. A pair of dominant objects, candlesticks for example, help to balance the grouping. Ornate frames and busy paintings may compete with the collection.

With today's relaxed decorating rules, you may group accessories with either formal or informal balance. Formal arrangements, which balance like objects, work well with traditional interiors, while an informal mix of accessories is suitable for more eclectic settings.

For an American Colonial ambience, a country-style print in a decorated wooden frame hangs above the painted mantel. Porcelain roosters and simple white candles in hurricane lamps set a warm, cozy mood. The mantel was painted the same color as the walls, a decorating technique common to Colonial times; this informal treatment is especially appropriate for a casual living room.

Twisted twigs in a cloisonné vase impart contemporary flair to this mantel arrangement. Crystal candlesticks and a torchère-style sconce lighten the look.

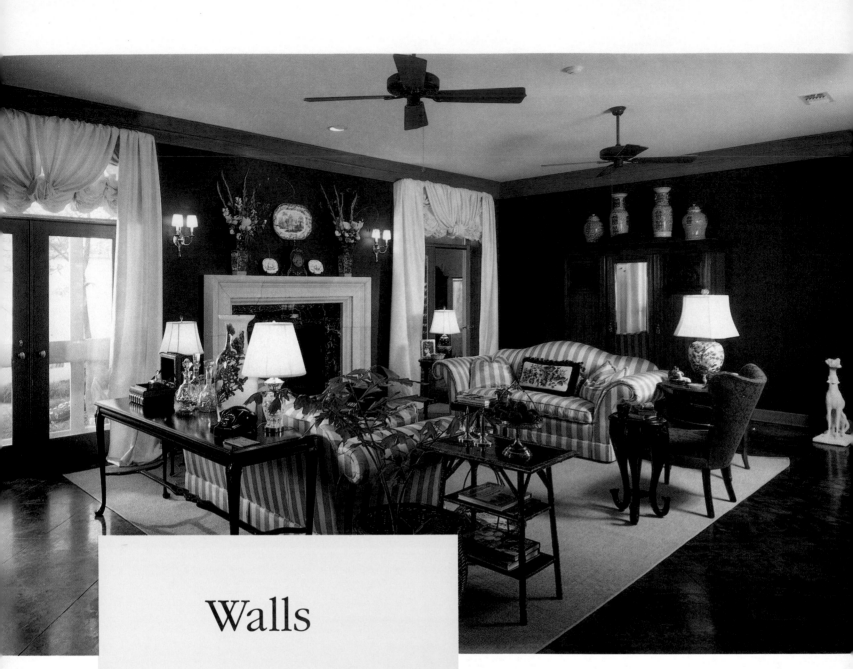

Walls

Never underestimate the power of color. Color is the quickest and most economical way to create interest in a room. The bold, aggressive use of color can set the tone for an entire decorating scheme. Color has the ability to affect space visually. Color can make a small space look larger or can camouflage bad proportions.

Warm colors—reds, oranges, and yellows—make spaces feel cozy and pleasant, while cool colors—greens, blues, and violets—provide a feeling of spaciousness. Grays, black, and white are neutral in relation to the warm-cool range. The neutral grays and tans make good background colors. They are easy to live with over long periods and have a subtle elegance. Whites add a crisp, bright feeling, and black is important as a powerful accent color. Bold colors create an atmosphere that is vibrant and active.

The stained and scored concrete floor and dark blue walls provide a sleek, sophisticated setting for this eclectic living room. A custom area rug defines the symmetrical furniture arrangement. Two camelback sofas provide ample seating.

A bright quilt and shawl add color and a casual flair to this white-on-white decorating scheme. The white walls and ceiling emphasize the rich texture and detail of the fireplace.

Deep teal walls contrast with bright
white trim in this traditional living
room. The glass coffee table and
kilim rug relax the formality.

Painted to resemble stone with
paneling above, this faux finish
blends subtle color variations
for an intriguing look.

Using the same color for the ceiling and walls, or a color that is a few shades lighter or darker, creates a monochromatic scheme and lends continuity to spaces—an especially desirable effect in odd-shaped rooms. Similar neutral tones on the ceiling, floor, and walls also work well to make narrow rooms appear larger and less crowded.

Dark colors add richness and intensity to a wide range of decorating styles. Depending on the shade you choose, deep color can create a sense of tranquility or a hint of drama. Dark walls can dramatize moldings, fireplaces, and windows. Attention can then be focused on unique architectural details by painting them white. In order to disguise awkward architectural elements, paint the walls and woodwork the same dark color.

One of the most difficult aspects of changing to a dark wall color is finding the right shade. The secret to getting the perfect color for your walls is experimentation. Buy the least amount of paint possible when you start. Begin with a lighter shade of the color and then go darker and darker until you find the one that works. Having an upholstery fabric or accessory to build around makes the color selection process easier. Paint several test areas on a wall; then choose the one that matches the fabric most closely.

If you feel that a deep wall color will make a room seem too somber, use light-colored or minimal window treatments, keep the floors light, or mirror one wall to visually expand the room.

To add color and a subtle pattern to your walls, you might consider any of a variety of painted faux finishes. Sponging and marbleizing are commonly used faux finishes which contribute a warm, textured look to walls.

This handsome sponge-painted wall provides a dramatic background for framed prints and a console table.

Moldings

Stylized columns frame this opening. The addition of stock molding at the top and bottom makes the wall seem like an engaged column.

This elaborate molding is built up from a number of moldings, then enriched with soffit blocks and a Greek key strip.

Adding molding to a room with no architectural detail instantly introduces character and a sense of depth to the space. Wood is the most used material for molding. Softwoods (pine and fir) are usually available in two grades, a clear or natural finish that is free of knots or surface blemishes and a more economical paint grade. Hardwood moldings are also available, usually on a custom basis, from millwork shops. For a paneled room, the molding should be the same wood as the paneling.

Plaster molding, once widely used, is still available from specialty mail-order companies. Rigid foam plastic moldings are also available in a variety of sizes and patterns, including ornate, richly embellished designs.

Double arches, trimmed to create a panel-like detail on the inside, gracefully open the way to a sunroom. The arched openings repeat the shape of the French doors beyond.

A decorative corner block, rather than a mitered joint, details this door frame. Bolection molding, applied to the wall, frames two Oriental prints.

❖ Cornice molding is used at the junction of the wall and ceiling and should be properly scaled for the room. The recommended height for cornice molding is $\frac{1}{14}$ of the ceiling height. For an eight-foot ceiling, the depth of the molding would be about $6\frac{7}{8}$ inches; for a nine-foot ceiling, $7\frac{3}{4}$ inches; and for a ten-foot ceiling, about $8\frac{5}{8}$ inches. A cornice can consist of a single piece of molding, such as crown molding, or be built up from several strips of molding. If the existing molding is too shallow, an easy way to add depth is to attach a strip of molding to the wall at the correct depth and paint that molding, the narrow strip of wall above, and the existing cornice molding the same trim color.

❖ Panel molding, also called bolection molding, is used to create a panel effect on walls. Each panel is assembled much like an empty picture frame and attached directly to the wall. If the wall has a chair rail, bolection molding can be used to form panels above or below it.

❖ Chair rails are strips of molding that run horizontally around a room thirty-two to forty-two inches above the floor. The chair rail (sometimes called a dado cap) serves the functional purpose of protecting the wall from chair backs. The chair rail also serves as the top of the wainscoting. Even if paneling is not used below the chair rail for a wainscot effect, there is often a change in wall finish at the chair rail. For example, the wall below the rail might be painted, while the wall above is papered.

❖ Base molding forms the junction between the floor and wall and helps protect the wall. The baseboard, too, should be in proportion to the room. For an eight-foot ceiling, a three- to four-inch high baseboard should be used; for a nine-foot ceiling, a five- to six-inch baseboard. The baseboard can be a single piece of molding or built up from several pieces. A base shoe is used to protect the baseboard and to cover any gaps. Usually this strip is finished to match the hardwood floor of the room.

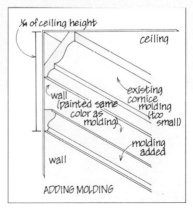

$\frac{1}{14}$ of ceiling height

ceiling

wall (painted same color as molding)

existing cornice molding (too small)

molding added

wall

ADDING MOLDING

Floors

The majority of wood floor installations, over ninety percent, are oak, and with good reason. Oak is hard, durable, and takes stains well. Most installations are red oak, which is more economical than white oak. Other commonly used hardwoods are northern walnut, maple, pecan, ash, elm, and chestnut.

Pine is the most common softwood used for floors. Though salvaged heart pine floors are prized, new soft pine floors can be bleached or stained as well. New Southern yellow pine bleaches and pickles easily.

Stains, seals, and finishes give wood floors their beauty. Wood floors can be left natural (particularly effective for oak), lightened (also known as bleached), or stained darker. Color can be added to the stain for a translucent finish. Penetrating seals, natural or colored, are recommended for floors because the sealers soak into the wood pores and act as a barrier against dirt and some stains. And penetrating sealers containing pigments do not fade in light, as do stains which are light sensitive. Sealed floors can be waxed. A sealer can also be used as an undercoat that stains the wood before the surface finish is applied.

A light look can be achieved with a combination of bleaching and pickling,

sometimes called whitewashing. After the floor is bleached to remove color, a special white stain made for wood is applied. Lightened wood floors are versatile, blending easily with a variety of decors from country to contemporary.

Whether the floor is left natural, lightened, or darkened, the final finish, applied after the stain or penetrating seal, is crucial to a beautiful floor. Polyurethane, either high gloss or matte, is very effective as the final protective finish for wood floors. A Swedish urea-formaldehyde resin finish also provides good protection for wood floors.

Wide-plank Southern yellow pine floors offer economy and a light, casual look. Because pine is a soft wood, be prepared for dents from heels and furniture.

This custom-designed teak floor is banded with inlays of walnut, mahogany, and quarter-sawn oak.

Parquet floors are available prefinished or as raw wood to be finished on the site. A light finish imparts a sophisticated look to this parquet floor.

Pine readily accepts white stain, a process known as whitewashing or pickling. A top layer of polyurethane helps to seal the floor.

Raw oak can be whitewashed for a fresh, light look. Because oak can be refinished, existing dark-stained floors can be updated as well.

Strip oak floors, in a natural finish, give a classic look in any setting.

An Oriental rug enriches a room
and helps to set the tone for an
interior plan. Aged by time, this
antique Persian Mahal adds history
to a newly decorated room and
blends with the floral French cotton
fabric and the antique pieces.

Tightly looped Berber rugs make a
subtle backdrop for both eclectic
and contemporary interiors.
Proper padding is necessary to
maintain the shape of the rug.

Area rugs offer a wide range of decorating possibilities. Available in a variety of types, styles, and prices, these rugs protect floors, define areas, and enhance interiors.

Before you fall in love with the colors and patterns of a rug, consider the size. That crucial measurement will make a major difference in the way a rug looks and works.

CUSTOM RUGS

Perhaps the ultimate rug is the one designed just for your room. Though this tends to be expensive, it will give personal flair to your interior.

Custom rugs are normally planned by interior designers experienced in rug design; although favorite motifs or classic upholstery or wallpaper patterns can suggest ideas as well. Borders also give a custom look to area rugs.

Custom rugs are available from several manufacturers and can be ordered through interior designers and fine furniture stores. Normally, the design is selected from the manufacturer's library of designs, or the manufacturer may produce an entirely new design for a client or make the rug according to the purchaser's specifications. Each rug is priced individually. A rug made entirely by hand will reflect the cost of the labor required to weave it.

❖ As a general rule, have at least eighteen inches of floor as a frame around the rug.

❖ If the room has a definite traffic pattern, use one area rug there and another in the seating area. In living or family rooms, the standard is to have one large rug or several smaller rugs to define the seating areas.

❖ For dining areas, rugs should be large enough so the chairs can be pushed back from the table without going off the rug.

Handmade needlepoint rugs are prized for their intricate designs and clear colors. Because they are stitched rather than woven, needlepoint rugs are most suitable for areas without heavy traffic, such as a formal living room or bedroom.

DHURRIES

Economical and widely available, dhurries are used in both casual and dressy settings. These pileless rugs are woven in 100-percent cotton or all wool, though wool is usually easier to find.

Originally striped rugs from India, today's dhurries are woven in a variety of patterns, such as seashells, butterflies, flowers, and geometric designs. They are available in pastels and in bright, deep shades as well.

Kilims are flat-woven wool rugs, similar to dhurries. Originally made in Romania, these rugs are now woven in India, Pakistan, and China as well. Though many kilim designs are regularly spaced geometrics, colorful flowers are among the classic Romanian designs. Today, with the increasing popularity of this type of rug, the Chinese are weaving flower-and-bird designs in deep, jewel colors. The care and maintenance for kilims is similar to that for dhurries.

Dhurries need to be turned monthly. Shake or beat the rugs gently with a carpet beater every month or two. Never use a rotary carpet cleaner as it breaks the fibers of the rug. Even small dhurries should be cushioned with foam underpads to maintain their shape.

Immensely popular in a variety of decorating schemes, dhurries are flat-woven cotton or wool rugs which are both reversible and durable.

Placed diagonally over a Berber-style wool area rug, this small kilim rug gives color and interest. Kilims are recognizable by their flat weaves, rather than pile, and are usually darker than similarly woven dhurrie rugs.

ORIENTAL & PERSIAN RUGS

Building a decorating scheme around an Oriental rug is a standard design practice—and no wonder. These treasured rugs are beautiful, strong, and infinitely versatile in contemporary, traditional, and eclectic settings.

Popular in the South in both formal and informal settings, Herez rugs are woven in angular, geometric patterns. Deep colors always include shades of red.

❖ Only natural-fiber handwoven rugs made in the Near East, Middle East, Far East (including Pakistan and India), and the Balkans can be legally labeled Oriental. Handwoven, flat-weave rugs, such as kilims, are technically Oriental rugs.

❖ In general usage, Oriental rugs mean those knotted with pile. Machine-made rugs must be labeled Oriental design. When you fold the rug crosswise, if the knots are aligned and coiled around the warp threads, the rug is handmade. Extreme evenness and machine-sewn fringe indicate machine-made rugs.

❖ Historically, three different types of Persian rugs were woven. The classifications were based on location and were referred to as city, village, and tribal rugs. Now the same three classifications apply to other rug-producing countries, as well. Oriental rugs are divided into two main design groups: geometrics and florals.

❖ Rugs should be labeled by their countries of origin as well as style. A rug woven in India from a Persian design is properly labeled as Indo-Herez or Indo-Hamadan. You should never remove the original tag from an Oriental rug.

Oriental rug care:
❖ Always place a good quality petrochemical pad under an Oriental rug to help retain its shape.

❖ Use a carpet sweeper to pick up crumbs and animal hair as needed. Vacuum about once a month (twice in heavy traffic areas) with a brush designed for wood floors. Vacuum with the pile.

❖ Turn the rug end to end about once a year if traffic is heavy in one area. Otherwise, every three years is sufficient. If one end gets more direct sunlight, turn the rug several times a year for even fading. If fading seems severe, consider a protective window film or an awning.

❖ Have knotted pile rugs professionally washed and mothproofed every two to four years.

❖ Reverse flat-woven rugs yearly. After both sides receive a year of wear, have the rug professionally washed and mothproofed.

❖ Never store an Oriental rug in an unheated space. If rugs must be stored, have them properly cleaned, mothproofed, and rolled or baled in brown paper.

Windows

Windows are an important consideration in the design of a room. The proper window treatment can set the tone for the decorating scheme to follow. In addition to being attractive, the window treatment should also function efficiently. When planning a window treatment, consider the specific needs for each window. Do you need privacy or to control the amount of light? On many windows, you may simply require a decorative touch of fabric to frame a pretty view.

Floral chintz frames a pair of French doors against a rich green moiré wall. The shirred valance is attached to a four-inch-deep board and mounted just below the picture molding. The valance drops to the top of the doorway. A small ruffled trim of red polished cotton edges the valance. Pleated draperies on a traverse rod stack just past the doors to allow easy opening.

To adorn a pair of French doors, lush layers of cream-colored silk combine in a stationary decorative drapery with a working shade behind it. The shade can be pulled up so the doors open easily. The entire treatment is mounted high over the doorway, emphasizing the high ceiling.

❖ Unlined draperies should be in a solid white or off-white unless they are combined with sheers or blinds that will diminish the print or color to the exterior.

❖ As a rule of thumb, keep the window treatments across the front of the house similar. This does not mean the same fabric for each treatment—just the same basic shape. The lining or secondary treatments such as sheers or blinds will keep the look uniform to the street. There are,

of course, exceptions to this. Level changes or changes in window sizes and shapes can justify changing the style from window to window.

❖ Small, uninteresting windows in formal rooms can take on new importance with the right window treatment. Mount the curtain rod as near the ceiling as possible to add height. The rod can be extended beyond the window frame, too, so draperies stack just past the area of glass, leaving as much window showing as possible.

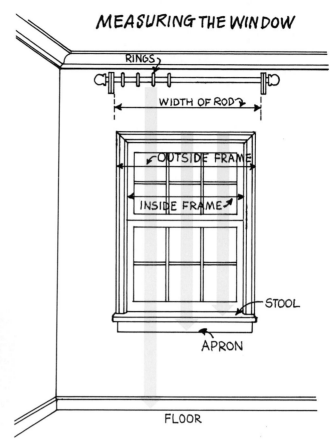

MEASURING THE WINDOW

RINGS

WIDTH OF ROD

OUTSIDE FRAME

INSIDE FRAME

STOOL

APRON

FLOOR

For many of today's window treatments, the trim and hardware become an important part of the entire look. Elaborate fringe and tassels used for tiebacks complement these multicolored silk draperies.

A Roman shade in a crisp, striped fabric echoes the wall and trim colors and adds a tailored look to the window. The rod pockets on the front of the shade make it appear to be layered. The whimsical bow-shaped valance is made from a single width of fabric caught in the middle.

❖ Unify different types of openings with similar window treatments. This is commonly done in traditional living rooms where there are both windows and French doors. A window treatment suitable for both is an attractive solution. Bear in mind that the treatment must accommodate the opening of the doors, which usually swing into the room.

❖ Selecting the right fabric for your windows is more than using a favorite print or color. The texture and weight of the fabric will affect the finished drapery.

❖ Consider how the fabric will look with light coming through it. Some translucent fabrics left unlined have a very desirable, soothing effect as sunlight shines through them.

❖ The pattern of a fabric is a cost consideration, because prints require extra yardage to match the motifs. Remember the larger the pattern, the longer the repeat and the more waste fabric you will have.

❖ For a full, luxurious, pleated or gathered effect, use a width of fabric at least twice the desired finished width.

❖ Install the curtain rod before measuring for a window treatment. A metal rule is more accurate than a fabric tape measure. However, a fabric tape measure is useful in determining the width needed for a swag. Drape the tape measure at the window to simulate the shape of the finished swag, then note the measurement.

❖ The proportions of a swag and jabot depend on the size of the window. No swag should be wider than forty inches. If the window is too wide, use more than one swag. The drop for a swag is usually from fifteen to twenty inches. The jabot or cascade should be about one-third the window or drapery length, or it should fall at a point of interest, such as the wainscoting on the surrounding wall.

81

Wooden shutters never go out of style, and they offer the greatest amount of control for light and privacy. Once installed, they become a part of the architectural detailing in the room.

Lace sheers hung from cafe rods mounted to French doors give privacy without having to close the pleated draperies. The lace is a soft complement to the printed floral fabric of the draperies.

For a subtle window covering that blends with the room, keep it simple and repeat the wall or trim color. Note how the shade is mounted, leaving the fanlight exposed.

❖ Swags hang prettier if they are cut on the diagonal. Keep this in mind when selecting fabrics. It means strong directional fabrics, such as stripes, will run at an angle.

❖ Many of the new relaxed window treatments use only a length of fabric draped around a pole or tacked to the window frame. These are stationary, so consider combining this type of treatment with a secondary backup, such as blinds, sheers, or a working shade.

❖ Full-length treatments that are casually draped look better if they are hemmed too long and allowed to puddle on the floor. It is difficult to achieve a precise hem on this type of drapery.

❖ Correct length is important. If the draperies are not designed to puddle on the floor, they usually hang to the window sill, apron, or to the floor. Allow ⅜ of an inch for the curtains to clear the sill or floor.

❖ Balloon shades are beautiful when they are pulled up, but for a working shade that will be lowered regularly, allow enough length to leave a small amount of "bunching" at the bottom when the shade is lowered.

❖ A balloon shade on a window or door where the rings, tape, and hardware are clearly visible from the exterior may not be desirable.

❖ Hardware and trim play an important role in the finished appearance of many window treatments. A bit of trim can add a vivid accent color, while tiebacks, curtain rods, and finials enhance the look.

ACCENTS

Left unframed, this oil painting is simply leaned against the wall, creating a dramatic backdrop for a collection of lead soldiers.

A custom-designed floor lamp is a unique accent in this contemporary setting. The lamp is a marble ball set into a cast column. The contemporary-style shade adds width for a perfect balance.

Print and solid pillows in primary colors add a vivid complement to a white sofa. Accents like these can be easily and economically changed with the season.

This informal mix of objects is formally balanced. The bowl with twigs visually evens the weight of the brass lamp, and the lid on the small box is left open for added height.

Two glass blocks topped with granite form a unique base for a pottery vase. Elevating a single piece of art on a base adds importance to the display.

A fringed scarf, laid on the diagonal, softens this antique American side table. A wicker trunk, topped with books, fills the space underneath to avoid the leggy look of tall tables.

GRACIOUS DINING

*T*he dining room is the most formal room in the house. A place of elegance and richness, comfort and style, this room provides the setting for special occasions from formal entertaining to comfortable family dinners.

DINING AREAS

A dressy, yet comfortable dining area provides a welcome respite from the frenzied routine of everyday life. The quiet, calm atmosphere of a well-appointed dining room is the perfect foil for the too frequent meal-on-the-go. The way you decorate and furnish your dining area is an important step in creating the desired ambience.

Matching dining room furniture is only one choice in furnishing your room. For a look with a lot of design flexibility, consider mixing furniture pieces. Combining styles offers several advantages. By having a potpourri of styles, you can use different kinds of tabletop arrangements to produce looks ranging from country fresh and simple to extravagantly elegant and grand, depending on the occasion. If all furniture pieces match, it is more difficult to achieve a variety of different looks.

In addition to flexibility of style, there is greater leeway for decorating around the furniture. A change of draperies, rugs, and upholstery fabrics can revamp the look of the entire room. With a matched dining set, you are limited to the fabric and window treatments that are appropriate to the style of that set.

Another advantage of mixing dining room furniture is that it allows you to buy pieces at different times and from a variety of places. You can mix a set of new chairs with an antique table or vice versa. This method also allows you the opportunity to find just the right piece for a particular wall or corner in your dining room.

Accessories and accent pieces can add dramatic flair to the dining room. For a small dining table, diminutive rosebuds or a few wildflowers make a lovely statement in individual bud vases. Handsome candlesticks with paper shades are beautiful accent pieces and contribute a subtle glow without overwhelming the table.

Deep red walls and a fireplace create an inviting atmosphere in this dining room. In keeping with the formal look, draperies are attached under the fixed cornice, while deep crown molding forms a finishing trim. A picture light and full-size lamps add warm accents to the room.

A welded-iron base supports the glass top of this dining table. Chairs are antique Sheraton. The Sheraton-style, turn-of-the-century sideboard is topped by a Chippendale-style mirror. Fresh-cut flowers in clear vases add sunny appeal to the dining room, while the fabric table runner contributes a splash of color to the table setting.

Transoms added above the double-hung windows bring additional light into this dining room. A mirrored wall seemingly doubles the size of the room.

Tables & Chairs

Shapes, sizes, and styles . . . the choices are limitless when it comes to selecting the table and chairs for a dining room.

Chairs upholstered in a flame-stitch fabric add a touch of grandeur to this dining room. The Oriental rug inspires a lovely palette of colors as a basis for the decorating scheme for the room.

In this easy-going dining room, a glass-topped bamboo table mixes easily with wing chairs covered in a crisp, striped cotton. Wall sconces, recessed lighting, and a shaded iron chandelier contribute to the room's brightness.

❖ Match the table to the size of the room. Be sure that there is enough clearance around the table for the dining chairs and for circulation. Allow a minimum of thirty-two inches from the table edge to the nearest wall or piece of furniture. This will provide room to pull back the dining chair and sit down. For circulation around the table with seated guests, allow forty-two to forty-eight inches from the table edge to the nearest obstruction.

❖ The table size depends on the number of guests you wish to seat. Allow a minimum of twenty-four inches along the side of the table for each guest. If someone is to be seated at the end of the table, allow an additional sixteen inches at the end. Leaf tables are an excellent choice for dining, since they can be adjusted in size to accommodate the number of guests.

❖ If you are using antique chairs, a complete matching set could be very costly and difficult to find, as well. Instead, try several chairs of the same general style, but with slight variations. Chairs are generally easier to find in sets of four.

❖ You can use extra dining chairs as occasional chairs in the living room; or, if you need additional dining chairs, use chairs from other rooms, as long as the seats are eighteen to nineteen inches off the floor.

❖ As an alternative to matching armchairs for the host and hostess, use upholstered chairs. All chairs should seat guests at the same height.

❖ You may choose to mix dining room chair styles. For example, at a round table every other chair could be a Queen Anne, with an upholstered chair of a compatible style in between.

❖ Round tables offer an alternative to the usual rectangular table. One particular advantage is that a round table can accommodate an uneven number of guests more easily. Some suggested sizes for round tables: thirty-six inches in diameter to accommodate four people, forty-two to forty-eight inches for six, and fifty-two to sixty-eight inches for eight.

❖ If you are making your own table using a glass top, make sure that the base will support the top without wobbling or rocking.

❖ An inexpensive table, such as one from a restaurant supply house, topped with a full-length cloth skirt is a low-cost alternative to a dining table. Some tables are available with folding legs for easy storage.

Two round dining tables allow two conversation groups in this large room. Chippendale-style garden chairs are painted a bright white; their colorful upholstered seats reinforce the room's crisp, fresh design.

An Italian olive jug forms a unique table base. The octagonal glass top has a beveled edge for a nice finishing touch. French-style chairs are upholstered in deep green leather to match the table base.

94

Pedestals with Ionic capitals support this dining table's glass top. The upholstered seats of the reproduction shield-back dining chairs and the deep blue wall color complement the large Herez rug.

Cupboards & Sideboards

Cupboards and sideboards are a versatile solution to the problem of too little storage space in the dining room. Not only do these furniture pieces provide attractive storage space for linens, holiday dinnerware, and silver pieces that are used only on special occasions, they also serve as display areas for your treasured collections.

❖ Corner cupboards, either free-standing or built-in, provide ample storage without cutting the room's floor space—an important consideration in a small dining room.

❖ Sideboards can be either a piece of furniture or a wall-mounted shelf. The minimum depth for the top should be twelve inches.

❖ A chest of drawers, borrowed from a bedroom, makes an excellent dining room storage piece.

This late eighteenth-century inlaid Hepplewhite sideboard offers an exquisite setting for lavish desserts. The deep red walls form a rich background for the dining room's antiques, including the nineteenth-century oil painting.

Cast griffins support a beveled-edge glass top for this sleek alternative to a more elaborate sideboard. A pair of contemporary lamps work well with the symmetrical arrangement.

A hunt board from Virginia contributes rustic, country charm to this dining room. Daylilies in a simple glass vase add fresh, lively color. A dough bowl underneath holds large pine cones and fills in the space between the hunt board and the floor.

A console table is a suitable substitute for a larger sideboard in this dining room. For entertaining, dessert trays and a coffee service replace the collection of blue and white china.

This built-in corner cupboard with shell motif richly displays a collection of blue and white.

Lighting

Since we use the dining room most often in the evening, good lighting is a primary consideration. However, good lighting does not mean bright lights. Certainly, you and your guests need sufficient illumination to see the meal, but a warm ambience can be created with a special focus on soft, subtle lighting.

Black shades reduce the glare from this brass chandelier. With the light from the chandelier dimmed, tall candles can add supplemental light for an elegant touch. A recessed eyeball fixture accents the mirror.

Four lights, recessed into the ceiling, provide ample light for the dining table. The use of recessed lights instead of a chandelier allows the dining table to be repositioned without upsetting the balance of the room.

❖ A chandelier is the most popular form of lighting for the dining room. When selecting a chandelier, be sure to consider the fixture in terms of the size of the room. A rule of thumb is to add the length and width of the room, in feet, then select a fixture that measures that number of inches across. For example, a twelve-by-fourteen-foot dining room would call for a twenty-six-inch-diameter chandelier.

❖ The chandelier should hang thirty inches above the top of the table in a dining room with an eight-foot ceiling height. For higher ceilinged rooms, the fixture should hang an inch higher for every foot of additional ceiling height. For example, in a room with a ten-foot ceiling, the chandelier should hang thirty-two inches above the tabletop.

❖ To reduce glare, small shades can be used with chandeliers. Available at most lamp shops, these shades simply clip onto the light bulbs.

❖ The chandelier, as well as any other lights in the room, should be on a dimmer switch. The switch allows you to control the light level to fit the desired mood.

❖ One good way to have both the ambience of a chandelier as well as plenty of light on the table surface is to combine a chandelier, dimmed well down, with recessed lights mounted in the ceiling near the chandelier. Spotlight bulbs can be used in the recessed fixtures for an even more dramatic effect.

❖ If you occasionally move the dining table from the center of the room, it is a good idea to have lighting other than a chandelier. One or more recessed downlights mounted in the ceiling near the center of the room will allow for more flexibility in the furniture arrangement.

❖ Secondary lighting in the dining room is important. Eyeball fixtures or wall-washers can be used to dramatically accent a piece of art or highlight a display of silver on the sideboard. These fixtures should also be on dimmers for better control of the light level.

Elegant and sophisticated, this dining room mixes a seventeenth-century Flemish tapestry fragment above the French fruitwood buffet with a carved ram's head from Italy.

A clip-on picture light brightens both the painting and the small chest below, providing an attractive focal point in the dining room.

ACCENTS

Since the dining table is such a large surface, it visually benefits from some sort of adornment year-round. A large covered casserole or tureen is an excellent choice for a centerpiece and can reflect the season easily when embellished with fresh flowers or seasonal foliage. This antique English piece, arranged with silver candlesticks, makes a stunning centerpiece on a large round table.

An acrylic base supports this silver domed lid, turned upside down and filled with blooming flowers and ferns. Moss adds a woodland feel and hides the soil.

Adding a stand or base lends importance to a tabletop display. A silver bowl, turned upside down, forms the base for a piece of handmade pottery. Crystal candlesticks are a fitting complement to the glass-top dining table.

Follow the season. Use flowers and foliage from your own yard for a delightfully fresh centerpiece. For special occasions, supplement your arrangement with flowers from the florist. Here, small, live azalea plants fill a large, glazed basket for a simply beautiful arrangement.

A delicate fern becomes an elegant centerpiece when arranged in a pretty crystal bowl on a mirror. Small votive candles add sparkles of light.

Use fabric table runners to add a splash of color to the dining table. Table runners also visually extend a single arrangement and unify different elements on the table. Here, tall stalks of Queen Anne's lace fill blue and white jars elevated on rosewood stands. The lavender table runner, laid with folds, gives color and protects the dining table.

SUNNY SPOTS

Greet the day with a cup of coffee, the morning paper, and the natural warmth of the sun. Entertain friends in a room that is bright and cheery on the dreariest winter's day. No longer enclosed porches for seasonal living, sunrooms are to be enjoyed year-round.

SUNROOMS

Today, we are carefully planning our sunrooms, siting them to capture light and views without excessive heat. Many new houses are designed with sunrooms taking the place of family rooms or dens. And older houses are often updated with well-planned sunroom additions.

No longer are they simply enclosed porches for seasonal enjoyment only; sunrooms are designed for year-round use. The fresh interior of the sunroom can complement the style of the rest of the house—from casual to formal, contemporary to traditional. Whichever style you choose, remember that quiet backgrounds—whites, neutrals, and wood tones—work best. With a neutral setting, the emphasis is on your furnishings, plants, and, of course, the view beyond.

Selecting furniture for a sunroom requires a bit of extra planning, since two or three of the room's walls are glass, and there is often a limited amount of floor space.

Bright, white, and open, this sunroom offers a casually elegant place to relax or entertain. The hexagonal tile floor echoes the white of the walls. The furnishings of rattan, bamboo, and pickled pine are all the same honey color. Puffy, white shades are set inside the window frames to allow the arched openings to show.

Arched transoms over French doors add extra light and elegance to this sunroom. The glass-and-acrylic coffee table helps preserve the light, open feel of the room.

❖ Consider how furniture will look from the outside when planning your sunroom decor.

❖ Coordinate the style and colors of the sunroom with adjoining rooms. There can be a transition, but there should not be a sudden break.

❖ Try to include a solid wall when planning a sunroom. The wall will be needed for displaying art and as a backdrop for case goods—desks, bookcases, and cabinets.

❖ If you have doors opening into the sunroom, either from the outside or from the rest of the house, be sure to locate furniture and accessories so the doors can swing open easily.

❖ A game table with comfortable chairs can be a welcome addition to a large sunroom or the sole furnishings of a small one. The table can be used for casual dining, school projects, and, of course, games.

❖ With large areas of glass and a hard floor surface, a sunroom can be noisy. Upholstered furniture, area rugs, skirted tables, fabric window treatments, and plants can all help to soften the noise level, while visually softening the room.

❖ To maintain an open, airy look, avoid crowding the room with too many furniture pieces. A small seating group—two chairs and a love seat—will need an eight-by-twelve-foot space, more if circulation space is required. Be sure to position furniture so that the circulation path does not go through the seating area.

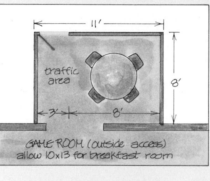

GAME ROOM (outside access)
allow 10x13 for breakfast room

Small panes of glass with individual muntin bars contribute interesting detail to a traditional sunroom. Framing the fireplace in fixed panes opens the space with innovative flair.

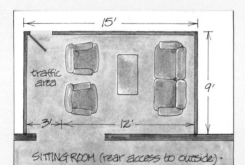

SITTING ROOM (rear access to outside)

SITTING ROOM (side access to outside)

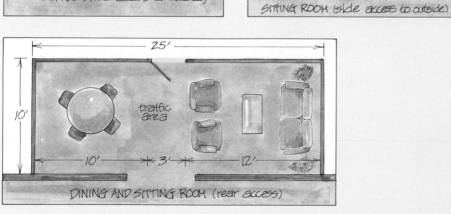

DINING AND SITTING ROOM (rear access)

Skylights

Light is what a sunroom is all about. If the windows in your sunroom are not as large as you would like, consider a skylight for the extra burst of light that can turn a drab space into a bright, inviting room. One of a skylight's main functions is to balance window light. A window can be glaring and uncomfortable if it is the only source of light, but a skylight eases that problem by adding light to the rest of the room. Even in a room with plenty of windows, skylights near the interior wall help balance the light. Porches, too, can receive similar benefits from skylights.

A border of slate edges this sunroom, forming a long-wearing path from the door to the rest of the house. Skylights along the roof ridge visually open the entire room to the outdoors.

❖ Skylights are either operable or fixed. The operable units, which are the more expensive, may be opened to help ventilate the house. They are opened by either a hand crank on a long pole or by an electric motor. Operable skylights are designed so they may stand open in a light shower, but they may let in rain in a hard, blowing storm.

❖ Another form of skylight is the roof window, which pivots in the middle to open on both the top and bottom. Roof windows are used most often in finished attics or rooms with low, sloping ceilings that may be reached by hand.

❖ Properly installed skylights, either fixed or operable, should not leak around their perimeter. Flashing should keep water running down the roof from seeping into the house.

❖ A skylight added to an existing home does have a greater chance of leaking than one installed in new construction.

❖ If you are adding a skylight, make sure that your homeowner's insurance policy covers water damage.

❖ Because heat rises, skylights do allow some heat loss in the winter. Double glazing helps eliminate the loss and prevents condensation on the inside of the skylight.

❖ In the summer, heat gain can be a problem. If possible, locate the skylight so that it receives a minimum of direct sunlight. Avoid the west and south sides of the house or locate the skylight where trees cast shade.

❖ You can screen your skylight to keep out excess heat while still admitting light. A lattice screen, either above the skylight on the roof or inside the house, will help, as will fabric shades or mini-blinds under the skylight. Some brands of double-glazed skylights have mini-blinds or pleated shades permanently encased between the panes of glass. The controls for the blinds are operated by hand, with a pole, or by an electric motor.

❖ Skylights also are available with tinted glass. Or you can add tinting or plastic sunscreening yourself.

❖ Angling the shaft that runs from the skylight to the room below can help diffuse the sun's rays and create more indirect lighting. Such an angle allows you to give the skylight its best placement outside (where it is unobtrusive, shaded, fits the roof structure), while keeping the opening where you want it inside.

❖ By flaring the shaft, you can have a larger room opening than the skylight itself and increase the amount of light in the area.

❖ For nighttime lighting, add cove lighting inside the shaft or mount simple globe bulbs on its sides. A lattice panel or other diffuser across the bottom of the shaft not only will screen sunlight, but will hide light fixtures.

111

Window Treatments

Painted wood shutters provide effective sun control in this sunroom. Frames for the shutters were added on the face of each door. Shutter panels also were inset into the frames of the transoms.

In some sunrooms, light can be too much of a good thing. So it is important to consider the type of glass that will work best for your room, as well as a window treatment that will control glare and ensure privacy.

Cotton fabric, shirred on tension rods, filters the light entering this greenhouse sunroom. In the winter, the fabric can be taken down to let in the warming rays.

❖ If possible, site your sunroom so that it does not get the harsh, western sun in the afternoon. If the room faces south, a roof overhang will block the hot, summer sun. In the winter, the lower rays still can slip inside to warm the room.

❖ If the location of your sunroom means direct sun, consider using windows made with low emissivity, known as low-E glass. Low-E glass consists of two panes of glass separated by an airspace and transparent metallic coatings. These coatings block radiant heat; so, during the winter, inside heat stays in, and, in the summer, outside heat stays out. A good choice is low-E glass with a slightly tinted outer·pane for heat and glare protection. Another option is bronze glass, which has a higher shading coefficient than clear.

❖ For a sunroom with operable windows that face west, you may want to consider woven sunscreens, which deflect heat and glare. The screens, which come in a variety of colors, tend to look less transparent from the outside than regular wire-mesh screens.

❖ If you plan to use double-pane windows, narrow-slat blinds, heat-reflecting narrow-slat blinds, or pleated shades can be sealed between the panes of glass.

❖ If your sunroom tends to get too warm, tinted solar window film is an economical solution. The film is attached to the inside of the glass to reduce heat buildup and fabric fading.

❖ Interior window treatments should be kept simple. You will want to be able to open up the room for maximum light and view, then close it off for sun control or privacy. Louvered shutters that fold back out of the way are a practical choice.

❖ Venetian blinds offer the range of light control of shutters at a lower cost. Blinds look best when mounted inside the window frame. Narrow-slat blinds are available both in stock and custom-fitted sizes in a wide range of colors.

❖ Draperies should be hung so that they can be pulled back completely, leaving all of the glass exposed. Shades, such as Roman or balloon shades, that can be raised completely above the window also work well.

Floors

The floor in a sunroom should be as carefree as the room itself. A tile or brick surface is an excellent, durable choice for flooring. As a bonus, hard-surface flooring will store the sun's heat in the winter to help keep the room warm at night.

A dhurrie rug placed on this Mexican tile floor defines the seating area. Skylights help to balance the light from the window wall in this long, narrow sunroom.

Ceramic tile floors require little maintenance, only an occasional vacuuming and damp mopping. No sealant is needed for the tile itself; however, the grout should be sealed for easier cleaning.

Brick pavers offer a durable, long-wearing floor. Protective sealant adds a glossy sheen to this floor.

❖ A major consideration in using ceramic tile is the method of setting the tile. Thicker tile (½ inch) should be thick-set in a ¾-inch mortar bed. Thinner tiles (¼ inch) can be thin-set on a ¼-inch mortar bed. Be sure to make allowances for the total thickness of the floor.

❖ Unglazed ceramic tile, called quarry tile, derives its color from the clay itself. Colors range from light tan to dark brown. The tile has an even, matte finish. If a glossy finish is desired, the tile can be sealed.

❖ Glazed tile is made by coating the tile surface with a metallic oxide glaze before firing. When fired, the glaze gives the tile surface its color and texture. Glazed ceramic tile is available in a wide variety of colors from bright to subtle. Surface texture can range from smooth to rough. Glazed tile does not need to be sealed.

❖ Mexican, or Saltillo, tile is a softer tile that usually comes in large squares. Mexican tile should be sealed, either before or after installation. Because the tile is thick (usually one inch) and somewhat irregular, it can be difficult to use, especially in remodeling. Some dealers do offer a ½-inch tile that can be thin-set.

❖ Vinyl tiles come in a variety of colors and sizes. Many duplicate the look of natural materials such as tile or slate. Because they are thin and can be laid in a mastic bed, vinyl tiles can be used where other materials would prove too thick.

❖ Brick is another long-wearing material for floors. Either whole brick or thin pavers can be used. The pavers come in thicknesses from ½ to 2½ inches. Brick can be set in a mortar bed or on a mortarless base. For paving patterns such as herringbone or basket weave, the bricks should measure twice as long as they are wide. Brick floors are usually sealed.

JUST FOR THE FAMILY

*P*at the dog, watch the evening news, play a game, help with homework. It is in our family rooms that we savor the simple pleasures of home.

FAMILY ROOMS

Practical and unpretentious, our family rooms are the backgrounds of our everyday lives. For households with children or teenagers, the family room means a common gathering place, an all-purpose room for everyone. These rooms welcome science projects, scout meetings, games, play, and, most important of all, just being together. When rooms stand up to this much activity, furnishings and fabrics need to be tough, durable, and practical. Likewise, accessories should be kept to a minimum —or at least safely displayed on a mantel or bookshelf.

Still, family rooms can be handsome. Luxurious Oriental rugs or dark-toned kilims and deep-hued upholstery can take spills and stains and still look good. And one more mark or scrape simply adds to the charm of rustic antiques and distressed furniture finishes.

Even if your family room leads a quieter life, it is still the ideal spot for informal living and entertaining. This type of family room may be used as a library, cozy den, or English-style sitting room. Fill it with your favorite collectibles and artwork, and it is a personal room that reflects you and your style.

❖ If the family room doubles as a playroom, consider making a play area behind the sofa. Furnish it with a child-size table and chairs and toy chest. An oversize basket for playthings helps keep the area neat.

❖ For a family with teenagers, get maximum entertaining space for both generations. A drop-leaf game table behind the sofa can be folded out for games, puzzles, or group projects. Chairs and a large sofa provide maximum seating while keeping an open traffic pattern. Large floor pillows, which can be neatly stacked out of the way, add more seating.

❖ Antique or reproduction armoires and cupboards conceal televisions and VCRs with style. Late nineteenth- and early twentieth-century wardrobes, made in England and America, are economical alternatives.

❖ Always take a tape measure when shopping for furniture.

Remember that antique pieces may not be in standard sizes. This is particularly important when shopping for an armoire, wardrobe, or cupboard to house a television, since the piece has to be deep enough to accommodate the shape of the set.

❖ Choose a floor that is comfortable and easy to maintain. If you use wood, seal it with polyurethane. New pine floors are light and attractive, but they dent easily.

❖ Consider tightly looped, Berber-style carpet for longest wear. Berber-style area rugs are suitable also.

❖ Use proper padding with nonskid rugs. Cotton rugs, such as braided, rag, or dhurries, are comfortable for young children who play on the floor.

❖ Oriental rugs with deep pile work well in the family room. The deep pile offers long wear, and the dark, intricate patterns tend to mask spills and stains.

A floor of old brick and exposed ceiling beams set a rustic tone for this family room. The contemporary oil above the mantel offers a contrast to the traditional furnishings.

A simple fireplace and flanking bookcases form the feature wall of this rear porch converted to a family room. Two upholstered chairs and a matching ottoman provide ample seating in a small amount of space. The green background of the bookshelves adds emphasis to each object displayed.

The high ceiling and exposed beams of this converted garage give this family room an open, airy feel. Animal heads combine with a collection of blue and white porcelain jars for an eclectic interior.

Comfortable seating and a game table add to the versatility of this room, which has appeal as both a library room and a family room.

❖ Wooden surfaces can be easily marred and dented. As an alternative to fine wood finishes, substitute distressed wood or stripped pine, which will not show scuff marks. Oak, a hardwood, works well for breakfast tables and desks. Older, rustic-style pieces, such as benches or children's tables, are practical furnishings.

❖ Antique or reproduction trunks make sturdy coffee tables, as well as handy storage space for toys, magazines, hobbies, and games.

❖ Look for new wood tables and chests that are sealed with stain-resistant, factory-applied finishes. A refinishing product also is available that includes a stain-resistant finish.

❖ Consider plastic laminate for casual dining or coffee tables. Laminates are available in a variety of colors to blend easily with your room's color scheme, and the simple style of a laminate table mixes well with both traditional and contemporary looks. Likewise, you may want to top built-in desks or dining counters with laminate for easy cleaning.

❖ Cover upholstered pieces in heavy linen, cotton, or blends. Dark, tightly woven fabrics wear well and hide spills and stains easily. For maximum wear, have a stain-resistant finish applied to upholstery fabrics. And if your room is sunny, consider using fabric that is specially treated to resist sun fading.

❖ Washable, cotton slipcovers are a clever choice if you prefer a lighter look. Slipcovers also allow you to change the look with the season. And slipcovers can stylishly unify mismatched pieces of furniture.

❖ Consider using laminated-fabric seat cushions for dining chairs if you have young children in the family. Laminated fabrics also work well for upholstered pieces if you have a backyard pool or a house near the water. A matte, rather than a gloss finish, is the most natural looking.

Family Rooms for Different Families

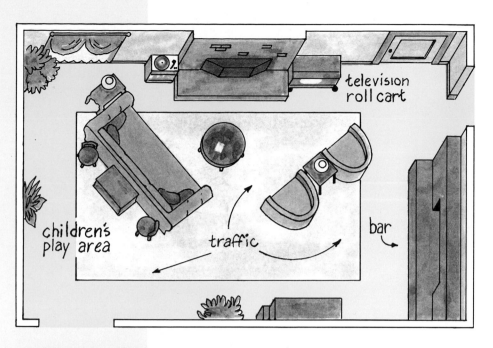

Comfortable and inviting, this room is a favorite place for the whole family to gather. Liberal use of reds, from walls to rug to fabrics, adds to the room's warmth. Nearby, the casual dining table is covered in a red plastic laminate. Antique hatboxes, a slouch hat, and a walking stick form a decorative display at one end of the couch.

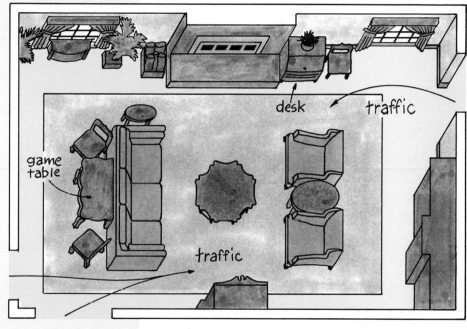

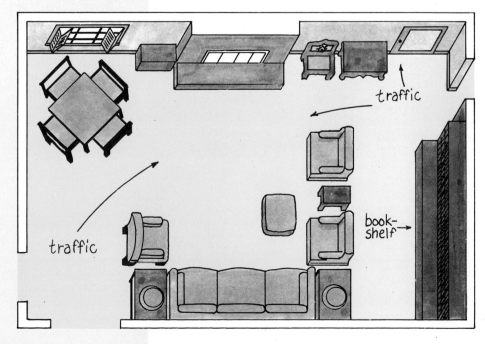

Painted Paneling

Painting is a quick and economical way to lighten a dark, paneled room. Pickling paneled walls imparts a rustic elegance to the paneling. Both techniques are simple to accomplish. Be sure to follow the directions exactly for the best results.

Stripped, bleached, and whitewashed, this paneled room is now lighter and brighter. The clear acrylic coffee table and light fabrics further the look. Eyeball ceiling fixtures can swivel to accent art and furnishings.

Painting:

❖ Properly prepare the surface so the paint will not peel. Use a household liquid cleaner and water to remove surface dirt and grease.

❖ Remove the gloss from the old finish by sanding lightly, or rub on a liquid deglossing agent, available at paint stores.

❖ Seal knots with shellac or clear lacquer.

❖ Prime with an alkyd-base primer. The primer can be tinted the same color as the finish coats of latex paint.

❖ Paint the prepared paneling with latex or alkyd paint. A semigloss paint is easier to clean than flat. High-gloss enamel can be used for the trim.

Pickling:

❖ Strip the finish from the dark paneling. If the finish was varnished, use a liquid stripping agent. A paste stripping agent works well for a vertical painted surface.

❖ Next, use a two-part wood bleach, available from paint and hardware stores, to lighten the wood all over.

❖ Add a small amount of raw umber to white enamel paint to muddy it a bit. Then, dilute the enamel with an equal amount of paint thinner. Add an equal amount of glazing compound to the diluted enamel to give the solution body and keep it transparent.

❖ Brush the solution from ceiling to floor, board by board; then immediately wipe it with a clean cloth.

Painting V-jointed paneling a soft cream color brings a more formal look to this den. The green of the mantel echoes colors of the marble fireplace surround.

Pickling unfinished woodwork:

❖ Brush a sanding sealer, thinned to one-half strength, over the raw or bleached wood. Allow it to dry thoroughly.

❖ Brush on a flat, latex undercoat paint. Allow it to set until smooth, but not dry, and wipe off. Oil-base enamel, thinned with mineral spirits, can be used as an alternative to the undercoat.

❖ Always test the entire pickling process on scraps first to make sure that you are satisfied with the results.

Built-In Storage

Built out from the wall, these shelves create an alcove for reading. Brass swing-arm lamps provide unobtrusive lighting.

Rich colors and fine woods create interiors that live well with traditional style. Books and collectibles enhance the warm, personal feeling. Built-in storage space offers a convenient way to display your favorite collections, while enriching the friendly ambience of the room. There are a few rules to follow to ensure that your built-ins are both functional and attractive.

126

Tucked into a corner, this built-in unit holds the television and stereo system. Hidden storage below offers a perfect place for games and albums.

❖ Books are heavy (about twenty-five pounds per cubic foot), so shelves must be strong to support the weight without sagging. The maximum suggested span for one-inch pine shelving (¾-inch actual thickness) is thirty inches. For extremely heavy books or records, the span should be reduced. For heavy loads or for longer spans (up to about four feet), many designers use ⁵⁄₄ lumber. Available at some specialty lumberyards, ⁵⁄₄ boards measure a full one-inch thick. For even heavier loads, two-inch nominal (1½-inch actual) or ⁸⁄₄ (two-inch actual) lumber can be used.

❖ Because of its stability, many architects and designers specify plywood for shelving. For painted shelves, ¾-inch birch plywood is the usual choice. Hardwood veneer plywoods are also available in oak, mahogany, walnut, and other woods for a natural or stained finish. The suggested maximum span for ¾-inch plywood shelves is thirty-six inches. For extra strength, two thicknesses of plywood can be glued together.

❖ Another way to strengthen shelving is to add an edging strip at the front and sometimes at the rear of the shelf. For example, a 1 x 2 strip glued and nailed along the front of a plywood or board shelf will help keep it from sagging. The strip will also help hide any shelf brackets or supporting cleats.

❖ When building a fixed shelf that will carry a heavy load, it is a good idea to run a cleat under the back edge of the shelf and firmly attach it to either the wall or the back of the bookcase.

❖ The depth of the shelves will depend on what you plan to place on them. Ten- to twelve-inch deep shelves will be adequate for all but the largest art books. For stereos and medium-size televisions, sixteen- to eighteen-inch shelves are required.

For paperbacks, shallow shelves, about eight-inches deep, can be used.

❖ Shelves can be supported in a variety of ways. Commercially available shelf brackets mounted to wall standards (sketch A) offer one of the simplest systems. A 1 x 2 edging strip will help hide the bracket; a recess in the shelf bottom will keep the shelf from shifting forward.

❖ Other shelf mounting methods

support the shelf from the ends, rather than from the back. The dadoed shelf (sketch B) gives the neatest installation, with no supports visible beneath it. The grooves in the bookcase side can be cut with a router or with a dado blade in a power saw.

❖ The cleated shelf (sketch C) is simple and strong, but it requires the use of an edging strip to hide the cleats.

❖ The adjustable shelf (sketch D) using holes and pins is inexpensive to make but takes care and extra time to drill the holes accurately. Bracket pins are available at most hardware stores. (You can use short pieces of ¼-inch dowel instead of bracket pins.)

❖ With the standards-and-clips system (sketch E) for attaching an adjustable shelf, the standards can be surface mounted, but the look is much neater if they are recessed flush with the surface of the sides of the bookcase. Again, either a router or a dado blade in a power saw can be used to make the groove.

❖ For additional storage, consider base cabinets with doors, using open shelves above. The base cabinets can be made deeper for extra storage or to accommodate electronic components.

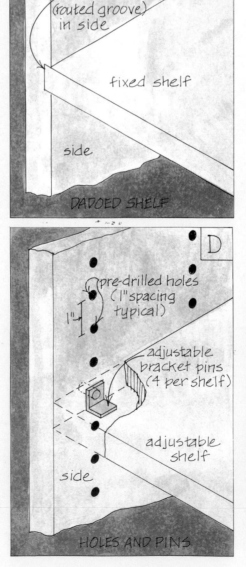

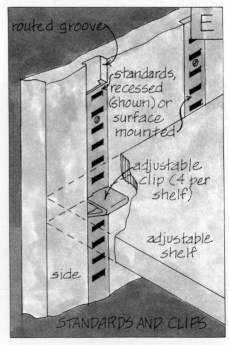

Employing otherwise wasted space, this corner cabinet makes a striking architectural statement. The inside of the cabinet is painted a dark brown to give a rich, neutral backdrop for the leather-bound books.

Window Treatments

Window treatments reflect the style of a room, while adding light control and privacy. Simple treatments that pull up and off the floor work well in busy family rooms.

A window niche with built-in seating uses the same fabric for the cushions and the window treatment. The balloon shades give a full look without intruding on the seating space.

Cream-colored raw silk imparts elegant simplicity to this window treatment. The fixed shade is not intended to be raised or lowered. The fabric panel is rolled on a dowel and is held in place by fabric-covered cording tied in a decorative knot.

For this window treatment, the shades are carried to the ceiling—above the actual window height—further emphasizing the room's spacious look. The horizontal lines of the rod pockets are echoed in the bookcase shelves.

Tables

Tables serve an important function in the family room. They provide a storage place for books and magazines, a work surface for projects and homework; they may double as the dining table for impromptu meals in front of the television, as well.

The coffee table takes harder use than most of the other family room furnishings, so a sturdy piece that will stand up to everyday use

is best. Special finishes, such as laminate or a clear polyurethane finish over wood, can add style, interest, and durability.

Skirted tables are a clever way to introduce pattern and color into the simplest design scheme. Table skirts are inexpensive, easy to make, and they can be changed easily to suit the season or your decorating whim.

This pine gateleg table can easily expand when a larger surface is needed. Books stacked on the floor add to the casual, homey feel of the room.

An oversize bleached pine table matches the scale of the overstuffed chair and couch. The distressed finish of the table will not show wear or nicks.

An antique chest, darkened by the years, is a charming, useful accent in this small, country-style room.

A glass top protects the fabric of this skirted table. The use of glass accessories brings lightness and unity to the tabletop arrangement.

Elegantly skirted in a polished cotton print, this round table provides a central focus for the room. Puddling the fabric on the floor enriches the look.

A quilted fabric, with the bottom tucked under, skirts this end table. A square of fabric, woven in a geometric pattern, forms the napkin.

❖ For a skirted table, use any small, round table or a stock particleboard round, in the desired size, with a pedestal base. As an alternative, a stereo speaker can act as the base for a particleboard round.

❖ Look for fabrics that drape but still have body. For a pretty, traditional look, purchase enough fabric so the skirt can puddle on the floor after it is hemmed. You may want to use matching fabric for accent pillows, seat covers, or window treatments. Or you can limit a dramatic fabric to the table skirt only.

❖ For a different look, use large squares of fabric stitched together for a patchwork effect; skirts with fringed or ruffled edges; or an overskirt (also called a napkin) over the first skirt. For quick decorating, use a quilt or large piece of quilted fabric and simply turn the ends under. Or you may choose to purchase a solid, round skirt and top it with one or more fabric squares to complement your room's color scheme.

❖ A glass round, custom cut to size, protects the fabric.

Posters, Prints, & Photographs

The family room is an ideal place to display beloved family photographs, as well as posters and prints from memorable family excursions and vacations.

With the proper artwork, you can draw attention to important accent colors in the room, and you can add emphasis to furniture arrangements or architectural elements.

The way artwork is matted, framed, and displayed can be almost as important as the art itself.

Art on paper—posters, prints, and photographs—is an easily affordable way to bring art into the home. The bright colors and strong graphics of a poster can brighten a room or accent a wall. Original prints include a wide range of sizes and techniques from tiny etchings to large serigraphs. Photographs, either as artwork or a visual record of your family's history, add interesting detail to any wall.

Sandwiched between glass, this poster leans against the wall for a casual look. The frame echoes the golden tones in the poster.

Four botanical prints, pages cut from an early text, accent painted wall paneling. The prints are mounted directly on the mat.

A grid of old, family photographs, simply matted, defines the wall space above a chair. Frameless corner clips hold the glass and mat together.

❖ Posters are multiples printed to advertise an event or show. Typically large and bold, posters are available at many museum stores and specialty shops. Posters are usually dry mounted to a rigid backing and then framed under glass. A narrow frame should be used to allow as much of the poster to show as possible.

❖ Prints are original art made in multiples. A variety of techniques can be used to produce the prints. These include lithographs, serigraphs (silk screens), relief prints (woodcuts), and intaglio prints (etchings, aquatints). Usually, prints are signed by the artist and numbered to show both the size of the edition and the number of that print within the edition. Prints should be framed under glass to protect the delicate surface from damage. Often, prints are matted to give a neutral area around the image.

❖ Frequently, reproductions are confused with original prints. A reproduction is a multiple photomechanical copy of an original drawing or painting. These are often sold in numbered editions, as well.

❖ Photographs can range from investment-quality images by a renowned artist to snapshots from your last vacation. Proper display can enhance the enjoyment of any photograph. A fine photograph should be protected by glass. Black-and-white photographs usually look best when displayed with a wide, white mat and a narrow white or black frame. Family photographs can be framed under glass or mounted in acrylic box frames so that they can be easily changed. Be aware that

color images are not permanent and can fade rapidly if exposed to direct sunlight. However, some methods of printing color photographs, such as the dye transfer technique, will produce longer lasting images.

❖ Any type of paper art is subject to damage. Unmounted images must be carefully protected until they are framed. To prevent chemical damage to the print or photograph, use only 100-percent rag paper or mat board. Be sure that the surface of the print or photograph does not touch the glass.

❖ Avoid glare-free glass since it dulls the appearance of the print. Proper placement and lighting of the artwork should reduce reflections.

ACCENTS

This glass-front china cabinet is an ideal way both to display and protect a collection of Imari. Small lights, set inside the cabinet, bring the Japanese porcelains to life.

A spray of tulips repeats the bright colors of a glass paperweight collection. Boxes used as bases for two of the paperweights contribute balance and height to the arrangement. Grouping small objects adds dramatic impact.

Clustered for maximum impact, this shell collection echoes the light, casual feeling of the room. Inexpensive clear acrylic stands give added emphasis to selected shells.

Silver frames unify this collection of family photographs. The taller frames behind act as a backdrop for the smaller pictures in front. Favorite objects and photographs add warm personal style to any interior.

A simple brass tray organizes this collection of bells. Arranging the bells within the confines of the tray strengthens the look.

IN THE KITCHEN

The kitchen is the heart of the home—the place where we gather as a family to share food and create memories, the place where friends become part of the family. The kitchen may be more complex now, technology has seen to that. But the dual role of functional workplace and sociable gathering place remains.

KITCHENS

The kitchen plan must accommodate the kitchen's varied functions and its wide range of equipment. There are many, many choices to make. Do you prefer raised panel cabinet doors, glass doors, or open shelves? Gas or electric cooktop? And what for the countertops? A separate breakfast room or a country kitchen? Sleek and contemporary? Or rustic?

Whether in design or decoration, these choices make the kitchen one of the most personalized rooms in the house and one of the most challenging to design.

White is probably the most popular kitchen color. It is clean, bright, and a good backdrop for all food and any color of china and cooking equipment. A simple background of white keeps even a busy kitchen from looking cluttered. Most white kitchens, however, need a splash of color for interest or a bit of wood or tile for warmth.

A small kitchen can be visually enlarged with white cabinets. These have traditional detailing, but the white paint adds a bright, contemporary look.

(Overleaf) Glass doors in the cabinets and a commercial refrigerator expand the visual space of this kitchen. A glass cabinet over the island seems to float in space. Narrow windows above the wall cabinets add brightness.

Despite dark walls, this kitchen is bright and open, thanks to white cabinets and a large, arched window. The white tiles on the island are repeated on the breakfast table. Even the ladder-back chairs are white.

Country and rustic styles—both American and European—are popular decors for kitchens. A kitchen in either style symbolizes hearty cooking and warm, pleasant surroundings, with the European offering a hint of the gourmet as well. These are friendly places where family and friends gather to help with the cooking and enjoy the results.

A more formal or traditionally styled house usually calls for a matching kitchen. Darker cabinetry, Oriental rugs, patterned wallpaper, and displayed accessories are among the hallmarks of the style—but not always. Lighter cabinets still can have traditional detail, and bright wallpapers can set a formal tone.

Laborsaving technology, design innovations, and an emphasis on decorating combine to make the kitchen an even more inviting place to be.

Traditional detailing makes this a warm and inviting kitchen, in spite of the sleek look of the black glass wall ovens and the hardworking commercial range.

Traditional details, such as brick walls and floors and stained cabinets, make a cozy, warm-looking kitchen; and they coexist nicely with such contemporary materials as synthetic marble countertops. Front panels on appliances match the cabinets and make the modern fixtures slip nearly unnoticed into the design.

146

CASUAL DINING AREAS

After cooking comes the eating, and whether for breakfast, a quick snack, or an informal family meal, the most convenient spot is near the kitchen. This makes both serving and cleaning up easier than using the larger, more distant, formal dining room. But it does not mean a breakfast or family dining area cannot be a special place. Design it with the kitchen so the styles and spaces blend. Keep the scale small and intimate, but avoid crowding the furniture. Make it a comfortable space for the entire family.

If a separate breakfast area is not possible, the simplest and most efficient way to provide dining in the kitchen is with stools at a counter. The arrangement does not require the extra floor space that a table needs, making it ideal for a small kitchen. And when pushed in, the stools virtually disappear. (If they have no backs, they can fit under the counter entirely.) Making a kneehole for stools extends the counter, so the kitchen gets extra work space. And even if the breakfast area has a table already, you can still use stools at a counter nearby for additional informal seating.

This spacious area incorporates the kitchen, breakfast area, and family room into one comfortable living space. The round table also can be used for games or other family activities.

Painted metal chairs, botanical prints, and a black-and-white tile floor bring a decidedly European look to this breakfast room.

This bright breakfast room sits to one end of the kitchen. A leaded glass transom delicately caps the cased opening between the living room and the breakfast area.

*A counter with stools is a favorite spot
for children to eat. For snacks or
quick meals, it is handy for the entire
family. The natural finish stools blend
with the light cabinets.*

The clean, simple lines of the table and chairs offer a touch of both the traditional and the contemporary, just as the kitchen does in this remodeled home. The sink serves both the kitchen and the breakfast room in this arrangement.

A large paned, contemporary window calls for contemporary furnishings, but mixing in some antiques works, too. Here, chairs are both Windsor and Bauhaus styles, and a bold striped cloth covers an antique table.

153

Planning
Your Kitchen

The U-shape is one of the most commonly used kitchen plans. Counters and cabinets can ring three walls of a room or, as in this kitchen, one counter can be a peninsula. The fourth side is circulation to the rest of the house.

How do you use your kitchen? It may sound like a simple question, but in planning your kitchen, it is probably the most important one you can ask. You will need to consider everything from whether you entertain in the kitchen, to how many people will be cooking at once, to whether you are right- or left-handed. Because the kitchen involves such an investment in appliances and construction, you will want to make sure you get it right the first time. Correcting a mistake in the kitchen is not as simple as rearranging furniture.

Working with a professional can help assure that you get the kitchen you want. You can select from architects, interior designers, contractors, and Certified Kitchen Designers (a relatively new profession specializing in kitchen design). Before you make a decision, you will need to review the designer or contractor's past work, check references, and establish all fees and schedules of payment.

A very large island turns this one-wall kitchen into a corridor design. The resulting large counter space is ideal for preparing large meals.

The four most common kitchen designs:

❖ *U-shaped kitchen (with or without an island)—with cabinets and appliances on three walls*

❖ *Corridor kitchen—with cabinets and appliances on two facing walls*

❖ *L-shaped kitchen (with or without an island)—with cabinets and appliances on two walls meeting at a corner*

❖ *One-wall kitchen—with cabinets and appliances in a line along the same wall*

No matter what the kitchen's size or how you plan to use it, there are standard planning techniques to ensure proper arrangement. These techniques derive from the three main functions of the kitchen: refrigeration, food preparation and cleanup, and cooking and serving. Most successful kitchen designs are arranged around an imaginary "work triangle" with one of these work centers at each angle. The perimeter of the triangle should be no more than twenty-two feet and no less than twelve. A kitchen whose triangle is larger than twenty-two feet usually will be so spread out it will be inefficient. A kitchen with a triangle less than twelve feet often will be too crowded.

The kitchen work triangle does not limit the design of most kitchens. With the proper placement of doors, windows, cabinets, appliances, and islands, it can be adapted to any design.

Big windows designed for the view are an unusual element that forced this kitchen to sacrifice most of its wall cabinets. But it follows proper planning principles for the work area.

Because the kitchen is so much a part of entertaining and family life as well as cooking, planning is essential. The relationship of dining areas and other rooms to the kitchen is important, too.

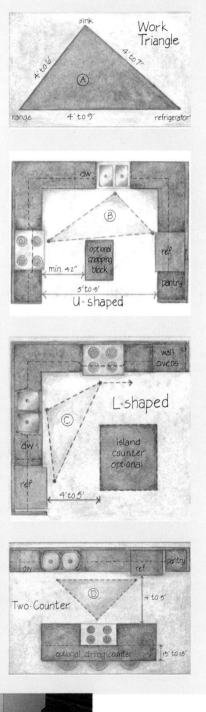

Two islands create a corridor-type de-sign that is freestanding in the room. Designed to be open for entertaining, the kitchen has no overhead storage, utilizing large cabinets built into the walls instead.

Even within the most common kitchen plan, there is plenty of room for variation. Do you want an eating area in the kitchen? An island? A desk? The laundry? Do you want big windows to take advantage of a view?

Before trying to squeeze too much into your kitchen, you must keep in mind basic space requirements; otherwise, you will not have enough room to work.

❖ In any kitchen, the sink should be four to six feet from the cooktop and four to seven feet from the refrigerator. The cooktop should be four to nine feet from the refrigerator.

❖ Wall ovens, where food cooks for long periods of time, can be outside the work triangle.

❖ Microwave ovens, where foods cook quickly, must be in the triangle and convenient to the refrigerator.

❖ The counter-to-counter distance across a U-shaped kitchen should be no less than four feet; however, five feet is preferable. If the kitchen has an island, the distance may be considerably wider.

❖ The distance across a corridor kitchen also should be at least four feet.

❖ To ensure ample work space, locate at least eighteen to twenty-four inches of countertop on each side of the cooktop.

❖ Include eighteen to thirty-six inches of counter on each side of the sink.

❖ Locate at least fifteen inches of counter beside the refrigerator.

❖ If two or more people commonly use the kitchen at the same time, be sure to leave extra space for clearance and add extra counter space. You may want to add an extra sink or cooktop, depending on the type of cooking you do.

❖ If you use a kitchen counter or an island for eating, it should have about twenty-four inches of space for each person.

❖ Such an eating area must be deeper than a normal counter, too. Leave twenty-four inches of the counter for a work area and eighteen to twenty-four inches as an eating area. Knee space should be at least twelve inches deep.

❖ A counter or island that is the standard thirty-six inches high will require stools. However, you can step the eating area down to thirty inches to allow the use of chairs.

❖ Tables also require at least twenty-four inches of length per person. To allow a person to sit at the end, the table should be thirty-four inches wide.

❖ Round tables can fit more people in a smaller space than can a square or rectangular one. Four people can sit at a table thirty to thirty-seven inches in diameter; five at a thirty-five- to forty-five-inch table; and six at a forty-two- to forty-eight-inch table.

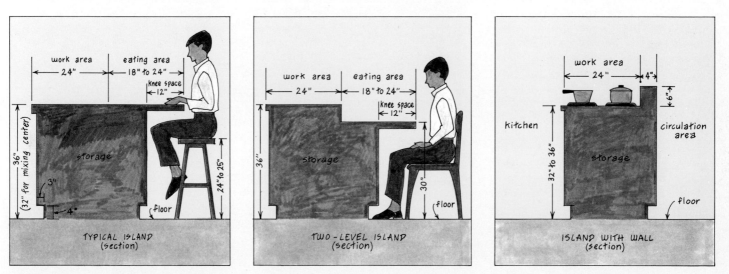

Planning a Kitchen Island

Cabinets & Storage

Cabinets are the furniture of the kitchen. Not only does their placement define the room's plan and circulation, but the cabinets themselves also determine the room's style and how conveniently it functions. Cabinets can be simple with clean, contemporary lines or ornate and full of detail. Properly coordinated with the way you cook, cabinets can put kitchenware and appliances at your fingertips when you need them or keep them hidden out of the way when they are not in use.

Stained, solid panel cabinet doors enrich a traditional kitchen. Matching panels on the refrigerator doors help the appliance blend into the room. The area above the wall cabinets is left open for display space.

Cabinets can be made to fit any nook or cranny for maximum storage. Cabinets in this remodeled kitchen angle under a staircase.

This glass door cabinet was custom-made to fit between two windows in this renovated kitchen. Glass gives the kitchen an open atmosphere and makes it seem more spacious.

❖ Kitchen cabinets are of two types: base cabinets and wall cabinets. The entire kitchen generally will be outlined with base cabinets (an island is essentially a base cabinet, too), but wall cabinets must be placed to accommodate windows.

❖ Unless you have open shelving, base cabinets always have solid panel doors and drawers. But wall cabinets

have the option of open shelving, solid panel, or glass doors. Open shelves are a casual look in which items are readily accessible; glass doors let you display kitchenware while keeping out dust and dirt; solid doors keep items out of sight.

❖ The recommended vertical clearance between the counter and the wall cabinets is eighteen inches

(fifteen minimum), with twenty-four inches over sinks and ranges.

❖ Including the countertop, base cabinets generally are thirty-six inches high. This height may be adjusted for tall or short people.

❖ Counters and base cabinets generally are two feet deep.

Contemporary cabinets are a striking contrast to the original brick walls of this old house. Small sections of wall cabinets fit between the windows.

❖ Base cabinets store large items such as pots and pans in their cabinets and small items such as silverware in their drawers at the top. They generally are twenty-four inches deep.

❖ Plates, glassware, and other frequently used items are stored in the wall cabinet, which has a common depth of thirteen inches. For easy reach, the maximum height for the top of the cabinets is six feet, three inches.

❖ You may add extra cabinets above the standard wall cabinets for infrequently used items; you may add a "furr down" to enclose the area above the cabinets with dead space; or you may leave the tops of the cabinets open to display baskets, pottery, or other items.

163

Cubbyholes for bills and home office needs are a useful addition to this counter.

A combination of solid panel and glass cabinets creates a 1920s look for this kitchen. Arches in the cabinets over the sink and cooktop make those work areas more open and spacious.

164

No one ever seems to have enough kitchen storage, and big cabinets alone often are not enough. If you want your kitchen to work, you need the right kinds of cabinets in the right places. Most kitchens need at least ten linear feet of base cabinet storage and ten linear feet of wall cabinet storage.

❖ The basic rule of kitchen storage is to locate items near the point of first or last use—glassware near the dishwasher, for example. You also must consider how often you use items, their size and shape, and whether you will want to display them. Open shelves can create an attractive kitchen and be an inexpensive alternative to conventional cabinets, but solid doors help avoid a cluttered look.

❖ Inside the cabinet, place items of similar height on the same shelf. If you have extra space, adjust your shelves so they are closer together. This will allow you to add another shelf.

❖ Add lazy Susans for spices or plastic racks to organize cups, plates, or other items on a shelf.

❖ To make corners more accessible, install lazy Susans in base or wall cabinets. Two-part pull-out cabinets also are good storage devices for base cabinets.

❖ Use shallow shelves for spices or canned goods so items will not be lost in the back.

Kitchen cabinets can include any number of specialized designs, from built-in microwaves, to wine racks, to niches for displaying pottery.

Drawers and open shelves in an island make reaching mugs and plates easy. The mugs rest on plastic mesh, which allows them to drain.

❖ Hang cooking equipment and utensils on a pegboard or a plastic-coated wire grid with hooks.

❖ Build into base cabinets spring-counterbalanced platforms for large appliances such as mixers. These lift up to counter level for use.

❖ Hide small appliances and countertop clutter behind "appliance garages," small tambour doors flush with the front of the wall cabinets.

❖ Install pull-out drawers inside base cabinets to make reaching items in back easier.

❖ Use vertical dividers to organize large, flat items, such as cookie sheets and trays.

❖ Use a flip-down tray behind a false drawer in front of the sink to store soap and scouring pads.

❖ Store seasonal items, such as holiday cookie cutters, and infrequently used items, such as fine china, crystal, or linen, outside the kitchen.

❖ Install can openers and other small appliances that mount under wall cabinets.

A rack on the inside of a cabinet door keeps spices organized. Because the space is shallow, spices do not become lost behind each other.

A grid with adjustable hooks is a convenient way to store cooking utensils. Shallow shelves provide perfect storage space for spices.

Countertops

After the cabinets, countertops are the element most responsible for establishing a kitchen's aesthetics. If the cabinets are white or natural wood and countertops are colorful, they will be the single most dominant element in the room.

But countertops are the kitchen's work area, as well. As a result, you must choose them carefully. The most popular countertop materials are: tile, plastic laminate, synthetic stone, butcher block, stone, and stainless steel.

Cheery hand-painted tiles accent this white tile countertop.

Synthetic marble is a durable material that gives a kitchen a clean, sleek appearance. The large piece on this island curves out on the back side to provide an eating area.

Like wood, synthetic stone, such as Du Pont Corian, can be worked into nearly any shape. The edges of this butcher block and synthetic countertop have been routed into the same detail.

A slate gray plastic laminate, edged in oak, tops this kitchen counter. The raised section serves as a snack bar and helps to screen the sink.

❖ TILE is durable, heat resistant, and long wearing. It offers a wide variety of colors and patterns, from solids to decorative hand-painted tiles. With a contrasting tile you can create your own design, such as an accent strip or other pattern. Finishes are available in a high gloss or an eggshell luster. Ceramic tile for countertops typically comes in 4¼-inch squares and six-inch squares.

Proper installation is vital for tile, which may be either thick-set on a mortar bed or thin-set using an epoxy-based adhesive. Grout between the tiles may be difficult to keep clean, but epoxy-based grouts, grout sealers, or dark-colored grouts make cleaning easier.

❖ PLASTIC LAMINATE is a smooth, easy-to-clean, inexpensive surface that is available in hundreds of colors and surfaces that resemble wood or stone. It is not as durable as other materials, however, as it will scorch or burn if hot pans are set on it, and it will scratch if you cut on it. Edges

may be a simple, right-angle self edge or a curved-post formed edge. Laminate also may be edged with wood to match the cabinets.

❖ SYNTHETIC STONE is a smooth, durable, easy-to-clean, but expensive material. Manufactured in ½- or ¾-inch sheets, it may be cut, carved, and shaped much like wood. Because it is a solid material, stains or burns can be sanded out. The material comes in several off-white colors, some with slight veining, and in a variety of granite-look finishes. Many edge treatments, including routing and contrasting wood or metal strips, are possible.

❖ BUTCHER BLOCK is made from laminated strips of solid wood, typically 1½ inches thick. Despite its origin and name, it is not advisable to chop on butcher block, as cuts will make it difficult to keep the surface clean. If you do decide to chop on a butcher block counter, seal the wood with a nontoxic oil and reapply the

oil every few months. A better method is to use a waterproof finish on the wood and chop on a separate, nonporous surface. Wooden countertops must be protected from hot pots and excess water, as well.

❖ STONE, such as marble and granite, is heat and water resistant, though it stains easily and acids such as lemon juice may etch its surface. The coolness of a stone counter makes it a popular surface for rolling out dough. The material is expensive, however, so it often is used only in small sections in baking centers.

❖ STAINLESS STEEL offers a commercial look that is durable, impervious to heat, and easy to keep clean. However, stainless steel will show water spots and is expensive to install. Stainless steel counters can incorporate an anti-drip edge, and a stainless steel sink can be built into the countertop as one unit.

Appliances

Cabinets, countertops, lighting, and decorating set the stage for what a kitchen is all about—cooking. For many people, the range, which combines the cooktop and ovens into one unit, is still the standard cooking appliance. But both cooktops and ovens are offered as separate units. There are other choices in cooking, too.

The cooktop is only a small part of this kitchen design, appearing as a black panel in the island. Downdraft ventilation eliminates the need for a hood that would intrude into the room.

❖ Though most cooks choose between gas and electric coil cooktop elements, there are other options, particularly in electric cooking. Some cooktops have cast-iron discs, known as hobs, which are raised slightly and are sealed to a porcelain enameled or stainless steel surface. Induction cooktops, in black or white glass with the cooking area outlined, are flush with the surface for easy cleaning.

❖ A popular option for people who entertain frequently or who cook for large families is the commercial range. These ranges are large (up to sixty-four inches wide, compared to thirty to thirty-six inches for standard ranges, and thirty-three inches deep, compared to twenty-two to twenty-nine inches), with six burners and

spacious ovens. They do require special ventilation, however.

❖ To ventilate cooking smoke and steam, you can choose between a fan in a hood over the cooktop or a cooktop with a downdraft ventilation system. Because downdraft ventilation eliminates the need for a hood, it is a particularly popular choice for cooktops mounted in islands.

❖ Microwave ovens and warming ovens are two convenience appliances that make cooking quicker and serving more convenient. Both are medium-size appliances (microwaves actually are becoming smaller in their outside dimensions while the cavity remains the same size), so they can fit easily among the appliances and cabinets in the kitchen.

❖ Refrigerators basically are types of storage, so it seems only natural that many are designed today to blend with the kitchen cabinets. Units with their compressors at the top or bottom are shallower than those with compressors at the back, so they fit neatly between the cabinets. Changeable door panels allow the insertion of sections identical to the cabinet fronts, so the refrigerator, the largest appliance in the kitchen, virtually disappears. Other finishes allow the refrigerator to match the rest of the kitchen appliances.

❖ Commercial refrigerators offer a sleek, stainless steel cabinet with glass doors that allow you to see easily the foods on hand.

❖ Sinks are available in both stainless steel finishes, which blend with any decor, and porcelain enamel, which is produced in white and a variety of colors to match tile, appliances, or other kitchen details. The best quality stainless steel sinks are eighteen gauge, with brushed finishes, undercoatings to deaden sounds, and nickel and chrome contents for durability. Porcelain enamel on cast iron resists chipping, scratches, and dents better than porcelain enamel on steel. If you have countertops of a synthetic marble material, you may have a sink made as an integral unit.

❖ Bowl sizes are available to meet any space requirement. Single bowl sinks (standard size: 22" x 25" x 8") are recommended only for kitchens with dishwashers. Double bowl sinks, with a total size of 22" x 32", are usually two bowls of the same size, but a wide range of other configurations are available—from two unequal bowls and triple bowls (the small section of each usually contains the disposer) to corner sinks, sinks with built-in drain boards, round bowls, and small sinks, which are handy for bars or secondary work areas.

❖ Faucets, hardware, and other accessories may come with the sink or be purchased separately. Faucets are available with a range of finishes—chrome, brushed bronze, polished brass, or metal coated with an epoxy finish which adds accents of red, yellow, blue, white, or black to the kitchen.

❖ Locate the dishwasher so that you can load it easily from the sink. For right-handed people, the best location for the dishwasher is usually to the left of the sink.

The refrigerator in this kitchen is covered with a panel to match the cabinets for a built-in look. Mounting the microwave under the cabinet saves counter space.

This cooktop has a ventilator at the rear so that when raised it draws smoke and steam out through ductwork under the floor. It retracts to surface level when not in use.

Flooring

Kitchen floors take a beating. They must withstand more traffic than most other rooms in the house, plus the spills and scrubbing that go with cooking.

But if durability is a major consideration in selecting a kitchen floor, so is design, because the options in kitchen flooring also are greater than in any other room.

Durable finishes now make wood floors suitable for the kitchen. Heart pine can stand up to wear and tear if properly finished.

❖ WOOD FLOORS—usually oak or pine—make an attractive floor that will blend with wood floors in the rest of the house. Polyurethane and the Swedish urea-formaldehyde resins can protect wood, though they wear in high traffic areas. The Swedish type can be retouched in worn areas; polyurethane finishes must be completely redone.

❖ CERAMIC TILE offers a durable, waterproof, easy-to-clean floor with great variety. It is a material that matches other typical kitchen surfaces well, particularly tile countertops. Most ceramic tiles are glazed, but some, notably quarry tile or Mexican tile, are unglazed varieties that must be sealed to prevent stains.

Some solid color vinyl tiles closely simulate ceramic tile, but because they are so thin, vinyl tiles are easier to add in a renovation.

Vinyl tile is a durable, inexpensive material that can be laid in custom patterns. This floor, in a 1920s house, is designed to resemble the floor of a kitchen from that era.

Glazed ceramic tile is available in a wide range of patterns and colors, or you can create your own pattern, such as this one, from different stock tiles.

Brick pavers are porous, so they must be sealed to prevent staining. Despite the material's slight unevenness, a well-sealed floor is not difficult to clean.

❖ BRICKS are another durable material for floors that must be sealed. Most indoor floors are made from ½-inch pavers, though full bricks also may be used. The pavers' length and width are the same as full bricks, however, and they may be laid in a variety of patterns, including the popular basket weave.

❖ RESILIENT FLOORING is one of the most popular types used in the kitchen. Though inexpensive, the thin material—in either sheets or tiles—is easy to install and is durable enough to withstand kitchen wear. It is soft, so standing for long periods while working in the kitchen is not as tiring.

❖ RUBBER TILE floors, also soft and durable, are more expensive than tile, and they give the kitchen a high-tech look. The nubby surface can be hard to clean, however.

Because no other room serves as many functions as the kitchen and includes so much equipment, kitchen lighting has to serve diverse and specific functions. One big fixture in the center of the ceiling will not do. Even if it seems bright enough for general illumination, it will cause you to work in your own shadow at the kitchen counters.

Instead, your kitchen will need ambient lighting for overall illumination, task lighting to brighten specific work areas, and mood lighting for dining or entertaining.

Lighting

Pendant lighting is an attractive way to provide task lighting over a work area that has no overhead cabinets.

A greenhouse window over the kitchen sink is a popular amenity, but a recessed light overhead makes sure the work area is bright night or day.

Fluorescent lighting below wall cabinets illuminates the counter work area. Lighting above the cabinets accents a display of plates.

ceiling fixture

WALL CABINET

BASE CABINET

UNDER-CABINET TASK LIGHTING

❖ To save money on electricity, cut down on heat gain, extend lamp life, and create different moods in your kitchen, install dimmer switches to control incandescent fixtures. You can combine cooling and illumination by installing a ceiling fan with a light.

❖ For general illumination, install either a central fixture or a series of recessed ceiling lights spaced around the room.

❖ Because cooking makes the kitchen hot, consider fluorescent lights, which give off less heat than incandescent fixtures. Centrally mount the fixture on the surface or recess it behind a diffuser.

❖ Incandescent fixtures, however,

are less expensive; and because they are smaller, they are easier to fit into a room. Since an incandescent fixture will not provide the bright, general illumination of a fluorescent, use several fixtures, either mounted on the ceiling or recessed.

❖ Some downlights provide general illumination; others have reflectors that also wash the walls with light. Keep in mind your own kitchen and specific requirements when selecting the lighting fixtures.

❖ For more focused, flexible illumination, use track lighting. Also use tracks in areas where you must light from a distance because you need open space overhead. Because they are surface mounted rather than

recessed, tracks are especially good in a renovation.

❖ If you have open space above counters or islands, consider pendant lighting. These hanging fixtures offer decorative ways of providing task lighting. In a kitchen with an eight-foot ceiling, hang pendant lighting twenty-four to twenty-seven inches above a work surface or thirty inches above an eating area.

❖ To illuminate counter work areas, mount fixtures on the bottom of wall cabinets. These under-cabinet fixtures are available as either fluorescents or incandescents. Screen the fixture so light does not shine in your eyes. Select tubes at least two-thirds the length of the counter.

ACCENTS

Canisters and tiles are functional items for a kitchen, but they both can be used for decoration.

Decorating a kitchen involves many elements, from large architectural details, such as this arched window, to countertops, cabinets, faucets, pots, and cut flowers.

Hand-painted tiles (this one is imported from France) add a decorative touch to the backsplash.

Cafe curtains are a natural for the kitchen window. These are sheer and pulled back to keep the kitchen bright.

Kitchen windows, often left uncovered to let in the natural sunlight, are ideal spots for plants.

Fruit in a basket is a simple decoration that is especially appropriate for the kitchen.

181

PERSONAL RETREATS

*T*oday, we design our bedrooms for much more than sleeping. The master suite is our retreat from a hectic world, as well as our private living space. Children, too, have multipurpose bedrooms that incorporate well-planned play and study areas. Our guest rooms pamper friends with luxury and sometimes serve double duty as sitting rooms or libraries.

MASTER SUITES

The master bedroom is truly a multipurpose room. It must function efficiently in the morning rush to dress and get to work, yet be a relaxing, and even romantic, environment at other times. The master suite may be required to function as a reading room, a media center, an exercise gymnasium, or a home office. Thoughtful planning will help you organize your bedroom to accommodate your specific requirements, as well as your decorating style.

❖ How the bed is dressed makes a big impact on the entire room. Changing the bed linens offers a relatively easy way to alter the look of your bedroom. You can follow the seasons with a light look for spring and a darker, cozier look for winter.

❖ Many linen manufacturers now offer bed skirts or dust ruffles in fabrics to match their sheets. When a dust ruffle is not used, and the box springs need some covering, a fitted sheet will do the job. Box springs are usually the same size as a mattress.

❖ For reading, you will want to have some seating in the master suite, either in the bedroom itself or, if you have the extra room, in an adjoining sitting room. If space is tight, a love seat will give more flexibility than a chaise. If you have the space, two comfortable chairs with ottomans can be used; and if you have a large sitting room, combine chairs with a love seat to create a cozy conversation area. A low table will provide a perfect spot for morning coffee.

❖ Good lighting is important both near the bed and in the sitting area. Wall-mounted swing-arm lamps are a good choice since they are easy to adjust and take up very little space. Down lights in the ceiling, positioned over both sides of the bed, can also be used for reading. Be sure to locate the switches nearby so you can turn the lights off without having to get out of bed. Table lamps usually are too far from the bed for comfortable reading. They do work well in the sitting area, however.

❖ If the master suite doubles as your home office, use a small desk or decorative table for your work area. Remember, though, that you will need nearby storage for files and home records.

❖ Storage space is always at a premium, especially in the bedroom. Often, existing closets can be reorganized for more efficient use of the space. For example, double rods, one above the other, can be used to hold shorter items of clothing such as shirts, blouses, and jackets. A tie rack mounted on the inside of the closet door uses otherwise wasted space and makes ties easier to find. Special sloping racks, mounted a few inches above the closet floor, can hold a second row of shoes.

Framed in steel, this canopy offers an elegant enclosure for the bed. For added richness, the fabric puddles on the floor.

*A skirted table and two chairs soften
the corner of this master bedroom.
Built-in shelves wrap the antique
chest-on-chest; the box above swivels
to reveal the television.*

❖ Because the bed is the largest
piece of furniture in the room, it
should be positioned first. The size of
the room and the location of windows and doors may limit the
placement of the bed. Be sure to
locate the bed so that it does not
block the traffic path from the bedroom entrance to the bathroom or
from the dressing area to the bath. If
possible, position the bed so that it is
not immediately visible from outside
the bedroom if the door is left open.
Try to allow two to three feet at the
side of the bed for circulation.

❖ If your closet is large enough,
consider locating the chest of drawers in the closet, instead of in the

An architectural fragment, swagged with fabric, forms a rich backdrop for this ornately carved headboard.

bedroom itself; or you may choose to use custom-designed built-in shelves or storage bins. Either way, you have all the clothes together, and you free up space in the bedroom.

❖ Provide plenty of storage space for books and magazines in the bedroom. Bookshelves, either freestanding or built-in, will give the maximum storage in the least amount of space. Oversize baskets resting on the floor can hold magazines close at hand; while a large table piled high with books makes an inviting display for any serious bibliophile.

❖ The television should be located where it can be viewed comfortably from the bed and from the sitting area. One popular way to conceal the television, yet make it convenient to use, is an armoire. For easy accessibility, the television can be mounted on a pull-out drawer fitted with a swivel platform. Old armoires can be converted by a cabinetmaker.

❖ A fireplace is a charming addition to the master suite. For a second-floor bedroom, a prefabricated fireplace unit eliminates the need for the expensive foundation necessary to support a brick fireplace. For a fireplace to be enjoyed from the bed, a raised firebox makes viewing easier.

❖ Exercise equipment, though not the most attractive of bedroom furnishings, must be located where you can get to it easily. If a separate exercise room is not available, consider equipment that can fold flat and slide under the bed or be moved easily to a nearby closet. A clear floor area for aerobics, located near the television, is also a welcome feature for the fitness exponent.

❖ In an older home, finding space for the extras of a master suite can be a challenge. If it is feasible, a small addition to the house could create an intimate sitting area for the master suite. Another possibility is to combine two smaller bedrooms to make a master suite. The wall between could be removed to create a single large room, or a large cased opening could connect the two rooms.

Originally two separate bedrooms, this master suite was opened up to make one large room with separate areas for sitting and sleeping.

Built-in cabinets wrap two sides of this bedroom, providing hidden storage and a counter. The marble-topped base cabinet functions as an attractive bedside table, as well.

A console table with drawers makes a perfect bedside table, with ample tabletop space for displaying personal treasures. In this bedroom, a round, skirted table provides a delicate contrast to its wooden counterpart. Soft, breezy fabric attached to the ceiling surrounds the bed, giving the illusion of a four-poster.

A narrow, built-in bookshelf doubles as a nightstand. A clamp-on lamp swivels for bedtime reading.

Bedside Tables

❖ A bedside table should be no higher than the top of the mattress; a table that is a few inches lower will usually look better and be easier to use.

❖ Bedside tables do not have to match. For example, you may want to use a low chest on one side of the bed and a round, skirted table on the other. Books can be piled on the skirted table for an attractive, useful display.

❖ At least one bedside table should include a drawer or door to provide out-of-sight storage of personal items.

THE BATH

Today's bathroom is a spa, a dressing room, an exercise area, a place to soak away the cares of the world; but it is also where you prepare to face the day. Only the kitchen has as many storage, lighting, ventilation, and other functional requirements. And no other room must accommodate them in such a small space.

❖ If you are building a new house, it is wise to locate the bathrooms relatively near each other or near or above the kitchen to keep plumbing simple and less expensive. Ideally, each bedroom would have its own bath, though in most houses, only the master bedroom has a private bath, while the children's and guest rooms share. A powder room should be placed near the living areas for guests, if possible.

❖ Whether planning a new bath or remodeling an old one, you will need to keep in mind basic dimensions and clearances for fixtures. The sink, for example, should have a six-inch clearance (two-inch minimum) from its outside edge to a side wall or another fixture and a thirty-inch clearance (eighteen minimum) to the opposite wall. The recommended side clearance for the toilet is eighteen inches (six minimum) though the clearance to the opposite wall should be thirty-six inches (eighteen minimum). The tub should have a six-inch clearance between it and any fixture alongside, with a thirty-four-inch clearance (twenty minimum) to the opposite wall.

Walls of glass block wrap the end of this master bath addition to give both light and privacy. The oversize tub was custom built of tile. Cut Mexican stone, laid on the diagonal, forms the checkerboard floor.

A raised, tile platform surrounds this tub, providing room for bath accessories and decorative objects. The secluded site and second-floor location of the bath eliminate the need for any window treatment.

A wall, pierced by a small opening, screens the water closet in this remodeled bath. A clear glass shower door and white-painted shutters on the windows preserve the bright, airy feeling of the room.

❖ In a large bathroom, you can divide the areas for different fixtures and uses into small rooms. Pocket doors add privacy but allow the bath to appear spacious when they are open.

❖ In a small bathroom, use partial walls or walls with cutouts in them for the same effect. A cutout or a half wall can provide a place for plants or display, too.

❖ The bath's largest fixture is the tub, which normally measures 2½ feet to three feet wide and 4½ to five feet long. Whirlpools and other luxury baths come in a range of larger sizes. Custom, tiled tubs can be made any size you desire.

❖ Showers should be at least three feet square to be comfortable, though they, too, may be custom-made in any size, with one or two shower heads.

❖ Because the bath often is wet, be careful in your choice of floor coverings. Tile is the most commonly used material, but if you want carpet for the warmth and comfort it offers bare feet, use it only around the sinks and dressing areas. Use tile around the tub and shower.

❖ Except for pedestal or wall-hung models, the sink usually is surrounded by a tile or laminate countertop. Leave enough space beside the sink for storing shaving supplies or makeup, and be sure that there is enough clearance—on the right if you are right-handed, on the left if you are left-handed—so you will not bump the wall.

❖ A pair of sinks—whether in the same base cabinet or separate cabinets—is especially convenient when two people share a bathroom.

❖ Generally, the height of the sink and countertop is thirty-two inches. If your sinks are in separate cabinets, however, consider making one thirty-six inches high (the same as for kitchens) or even higher for shaving.

195

❖ Lighting in the bathroom, as in the kitchen, must be a combination of general overhead lighting and task lighting. In this case, the task lighting is around or above the mirror. Use incandescent fixtures for truer flesh tones, and be sure to position the lights so that they do not cast shadows or shine in your eyes.

❖ Windows help freshen and brighten the bath, but privacy is more of a consideration here than in most rooms. You can hang fabric curtains, but you will need shades or blinds behind them that can be opened and closed easily and frequently. Mini-blinds are a popular choice in baths for their ease of operation and their ability to withstand the often hot, damp atmosphere of the room.

❖ Skylights are a good way to let in light and ensure privacy. They are especially useful in interior baths without windows.

❖ Building codes typically require either a window or a ventilator in a bath. You also will want to air the room as much as possible to reduce the possibility of mildew. Ventilating units, usually mounted in the ceiling, may include only an exhaust fan or a fan and a light. Heat lamps, either as independent units or combined with fans, also are popular.

❖ The bath's humid atmosphere makes it ideal for plants. Placed near a window, on a high shelf under a skylight, or near the tub, plants will flourish.

❖ For plants, storage, or display, shelves at one or both ends of the tub are a useful addition.

❖ For other storage, take a cue from the kitchen. The same sliding shelves and plastic-coated wire racks you use in kitchen cabinets will work just as well in the bath.

The routed edge of this solid-surface countertop curves for easier access to the tub. Sliding mirrored doors conceal storage space.

A built-in chest of drawers and a low vanity give needed storage in this dressing area. The entire wall is mirrored to visually double the space.

A marble countertop covers the rim of the white porcelain bowls for a sleek, easy-to-clean surface. Mirrored doors hide storage at the end of the vanity. Theatrical-style makeup lights mount directly on the mirror.

❖ Put an electrical outlet inside a cabinet so you can leave your hair dryer plugged in but still stored out of the way.

❖ Medicine cabinets, unlike the kitchen's wall cabinets, are shallow so they take up little space. They can be installed on the side wall or built in over the sink. If you have small children, you may want to have at least one cabinet or drawer that will lock to safeguard medicine.

❖ A large bath and dressing area also may have room for a small refrigerator and sink for morning coffee.

❖ In the dressing area, install an ironing board that folds down from a cabinet in the wall.

❖ If your bath and dressing area are on the second floor and the laundry is downstairs, add a laundry chute. In a new house, consider locating the laundry as close to the bedrooms as possible.

Built-in cabinets at one end of this bath add both hidden storage and out-in-the-open display space.

Built on two levels, this countertop is comfortable for both standing and sitting. The vanity bowl is cast into the solid-surface countertop. Thin-slat venetian blinds offer easy control of light and privacy. The floor in the dressing area is carpeted, while the area around the tub is tiled.

CHILDREN'S ROOMS

Durable, easy-care furnishings and finishes—and plenty of well-planned, accessible storage—are the top priorities when planning children's rooms. But how you actually decorate the room depends on how often you plan to redecorate. Hand-painted wall scenes and murals, stenciling, and wallpaper or wallpaper borders for children are delightful in a child's room; but remember that a child's interests change rapidly. Nursery themes may no longer suit your child's interests by the time he reaches kindergarten. Likewise, popular cartoon and film characters can quickly go out of style. If you want to decorate your child's room around a particular theme, however, comforters and curtains made from matching sheets are an easy-to-change solution.

For floors, cotton dhurrie or rag rugs can add a touch of brightness while softening the floor for a young child. Custom window treatments, such as tailored Roman shades, should be in neutral plaids or solids.

Fabric hanging from the ceiling creates the illusion of a feminine, canopy bed. The shades of the two swing-arm lamps are covered with the same print fabric. A wide, printed ribbon accents the fabric and borders the wallpaper at the ceiling.

Matching beds tuck under the eaves in this attic bedroom. An arched opening leads to a cozy seating area. Swing-arm lamps provide convenient, out-of-the-way light for bedtime reading. The pink-and-white color scheme is reinforced by the matching wallpaper and bed linens.

❖ Buy twin or bunk beds to maximize space. If two children share the room, this is a must. If not, the extra bed welcomes overnight guests. Twin and bunk beds are available in a wide variety of materials and finishes, including natural and stained wood and enameled metal. Antique twin beds, with brass or carved wood headboards, are also available.

❖ The most practical course is to buy basic, sturdy beds that can last through childhood. A child may tire of a bed in the shape of an automobile or ship, for example.

❖ Work with a designer or cabinetmaker for built-in or custom-made bunk beds. A loft bed, for example, can save space. Or custom-made bunk beds can incorporate storage.

❖ For extra storage, consider a pair of captain's beds, which have under-the-bed storage. Platform beds, such as these, normally use a mattress only.

❖ Consider stock or custom-made folding beds, sometimes called Murphy beds, if space is extremely tight.

❖ Use wall-mounted reading lamps to provide good reading light without the clutter of table or floor lamps.

❖ Hang a bulletin board so your child can display memorabilia such as posters, certificates, ribbons, drawings, and photos of friends.

❖ Simply framed posters, such as those purchased at zoos or festivals, or bright prints are ideal for the walls of a child's room. When a child reaches school age, frame some of his own artwork to display in his room.

❖ Use large floor pillows or child-size futons for extra seating.

Room for play as well as study is important to a child of any age. The antiqued finish on the bed will not show wear.

Built-in bookshelves flank this nursery alcove. When the child is older, a standard bed could fit between the units, with the head to the wall.

A child's bedroom is the perfect place to give tired, old furniture new life with a whimsical painted finish.

Converted from a closet, this compact study includes a built-in desk with a hinged top for extra storage. The interior of the closet was painted to coordinate with the plaid wallpaper.

A wall of built-ins provides plenty of toy storage for a preschooler. Later, the desk can be used for study. Plastic laminate offers an easy-to-clean countertop.

Storage Ideas

❖ The most traditional and basic method of storage in a child's room is the toy box. It works well for certain toys, but for such items as collections, crayons, school supplies, and small toys, a series of small boxes that can be stored on shelves or in the closet is a good idea.

❖ A desk can be built with a top that "grows" with the child. In a built-in storage unit, simply mount the work surface on adjustable shelf standards on flanking cabinets.

❖ Children's needs change quickly, building blocks and teddy bears soon give way to soccer trophies and

computers. When planning a child's room, choose storage and display systems that either can be adapted to new needs or that can be replaced easily.

❖ Toys such as stuffed animals or dolls that a younger child plays with will be items to display in an older child's room. Shelves are a good way to store them for either age. The younger child can find a toy on a shelf easily; the older one can keep it on view but out of the way. Adjustable shelves are particularly useful for displays that change with the child's age.

❖ File cabinets provide a good place to store school papers.

❖ If you have extra closet space, you can create a private study area by building in a desk. You may remove the door or leave it in place so the desk can be screened from the room when it is not in use.

❖ Because children's artwork and homework often involve paint, crayons, or glue, be sure the desktop is durable. Plastic laminate is a good choice. If you have a surface that is easily marred, protect it with a desktop blotter.

❖ Since children's clothes are small, you can install two rods—one above the other—in the closet for extra storage. A low rod will be easier for a child to reach, too.

CREDITS

At the time the photographs were taken, these were the owners. Architect and designer credits are given for the homes and rooms pictured, when available.

jacket photographs:
 Owners: John and Mary Allison, Little Rock, Arkansas
 Architect: John Allison, AIA, Little Rock, Arkansas
 Photographer: John O'Hagan
back jacket photographs:
(top left):
 Owners: David and Leslie Cox, Jackson, Mississippi
 Architect: Ken Tate, Jackson, Mississippi
 Designer: Charme Tate, ASID, Jackson, Mississippi
 Photographer: John O'Hagan
(top right):
 Owner/Designer: Jim Pfaffman, AIA, Birmingham, Alabama
 Photographer: Cheryl Sales
(bottom right):
 Owner/Designer: Ron Clemmer, Asheville, North Carolina
 Photographer: Cheryl Sales
(bottom left):
 Owners: Key and Jean Foster, Birmingham, Alabama
 Photographer: John O'Hagan

Chapter 1 – A STYLE FOR YOU
page 9:
 Owners: Benton and Cynthia Rutledge, Dallas, Texas
 Designer: Cynthia Rutledge, Dallas, Texas
 Photographer: John O'Hagan
page 10:
 Owners: Mr. and Mrs. Jim Freese, Tulsa, Oklahoma
 Designer: Charles Faudree, Tulsa, Oklahoma
 Photographer: John O'Hagan
page 12:
 Owners: Ferrell and Pam Scruggs, Valdosta, Georgia
 Architect: Frank McCall, FAIA, Valdosta, Georgia
 Photographer: John O'Hagan
page 14:
 Owners: Paul and Alix Rico, New Orleans, Louisiana

Designer: Alix Rico, New Orleans, Louisiana
 Photographer: Cheryl Sales
page 15:
 Owner/Designer: Charles Faudree, Tulsa, Oklahoma
 Architect: John Brooks Walton, Tulsa, Oklahoma
 Photographer: John O'Hagan
page 16:
 Owners: Bill and Nancy Grogan, Madison County, Mississippi
 Photographer: John O'Hagan
page 17:
 Owners: Mike and Genny Doramus, Dallas, Texas
 Builder: Bob Forrest, Dallas, Texas
 Photographer: John O'Hagan
page 18:
 Owner/Designer: Charles Faudree, Tulsa, Oklahoma
 Architect: John Brooks Walton, Tulsa, Oklahoma
 Photographer: John O'Hagan
page 19:
 Owners: Martin and Susan Kilpatrick, Atlanta, Georgia
 Designer: Susan Kilpatrick, Atlanta, Georgia
 Photographer: John O'Hagan
page 20:
 Owner/Designer: Charles Faudree, Tulsa, Oklahoma
 Architect: John Brooks Walton, Tulsa, Oklahoma
 Photographer: John O'Hagan
page 23:
 Owners: Mr. and Mrs. Wilson Mason, Dallas, Texas
 Designer/Builder: Bob Forrest, Dallas, Texas
 Photographer: John O'Hagan
page 24:
 Owner/Designer: Charles Faudree, Tulsa, Oklahoma
 Architect: John Brooks Walton, Tulsa, Oklahoma
 Photographer: John O'Hagan
page 25:
 Owner/Designer: Phillip Sides, Montgomery, Alabama
 Photographer: John O'Hagan
page 26:
 Owners: Benton and Cynthia Rutledge, Dallas, Texas
 Designer: Cynthia Rutledge, Dallas, Texas
 Photographer: John O'Hagan
page 27:
 Owners: Benton and Cynthia Rutledge, Dallas, Texas

Designer: Cynthia Rutledge, Dallas, Texas
 Photographer: John O'Hagan
page 28:
 Owners: Terri Finitzo and Pat Heiber, Dallas, Texas
 Architect: Max Levy, AIA, Dallas, Texas
 Photographer: John O'Hagan
page 29:
 Architects: Robert Hammond, AIA, and Jay Huyett, AIA, Annapolis, Maryland
 Photographer: John O'Hagan
page 30:
 Owners: William and Becky Ketcher, Little Rock, Arkansas
 Architect: Rick Redden, AIA, Little Rock, Arkansas
 Photographer: John O'Hagan
page 31:
 Owners/Designers: Noel and Leigh Harris, Greenville, Mississippi
 Photographer: John O'Hagan

Chapter 2 – FIRST IMPRESSIONS
page 33:
 Owner/Designer: Tim Hargrove, Oxford, Mississippi
 Photographer: John O'Hagan
page 34:
 Photographer: Bob Lancaster
page 35:
 Owners: Harlan and Jean Stone, Baltimore, Maryland
 Architect: Walter Schamu, Baltimore, Maryland
 Photographer: John O'Hagan
page 36:
 Owners: Johnny and Johanna Aiken, Greenville, South Carolina
 Architect: Robin Prince, AIA, Greenville, South Carolina
 Designer: James Clamp, ASID, Greenville, South Carolina
 Photographer: Cheryl Sales
page 37:
 Owners: Randy and Liza Bryan, Atlanta, Georgia
 Architect: Norman Askins, Atlanta, Georgia
 Designer: Liza Bryan, Atlanta, Georgia
 Photographer: John O'Hagan
page 38:
 Owners: John and Ann Marie Dalis, Augusta, Georgia
 Designer: Ann Marie Dalis, Augusta, Georgia
 Photographer: Cheryl Sales

page 39:
Owners: John and Sally Tinney, Wilmington, North Carolina
Architect: Jay Dechesene, AIA, Wrightsville Beach, North Carolina
Photographer: John O'Hagan
page 40:
Owners: Jane Keyser and Michael Krumbein, Richmond, Virginia
Architect: Charles Aquino, AIA, Richmond, Virginia
Photographer: John O'Hagan
page 41:
Owners: William and Becky Ketcher, Little Rock, Arkansas
Architect: Rick Redden, AIA, Little Rock, Arkansas
Photographer: John O'Hagan
page 42 (top):
Owners: James and Imelda Stevenson, Morgantown, West Virginia
Designer: Pat Bibbee, Charleston, West Virginia
Photographer: John O'Hagan
page 42 (bottom):
Owners: Wade and Sissy Brodie, Aiken, South Carolina
Designer: Julie Adams, Aiken, South Carolina
Photographer: Cheryl Sales
page 43:
Owners: Robert and Kimberly Myers, Belleair, Florida
Designer: Jan Hale Crawford, Belleair, Florida
Photographer: Cheryl Sales
page 44:
Owner: Sandra Jacques, Nashville, Tennessee
Designer: Deborah Tallent of Wm. M. Hamilton and Associates, Nashville, Tennessee
Photographer: Louis Joyner
page 45 (top):
Owners: Robert and Susanne Adams, Alexandria, Virginia
Architect: Robert Bentley Adams, AIA, Alexandria, Virginia
Photographer: John O'Hagan
page 45 (bottom):
Owner/Designer: Tim Hargrove, Oxford, Mississippi
Photographer: John O'Hagan
page 46:
Owners: Key and Jean Foster, Birmingham, Alabama
Photographer: John O'Hagan
page 47 (top):
Owners: James and Shara Overstreet, Augusta, Georgia
Designer: Shara Overstreet, ASID,

Augusta, Georgia
Photographer: Cheryl Sales
page 47 (bottom):
Owner: Tricie Cromwell, Little Rock, Arkansas
Architect: Ed Cromwell, AIA, Little Rock, Arkansas
Photographer: Ardon Armstrong
page 48:
Owners: Rob and Anne Couch, Birmingham, Alabama
Designer: Anne Couch, Birmingham, Alabama
Photographer: Cheryl Sales
page 49 (top):
Owners: Robert and Suzanne Chesnut, Charleston, South Carolina
Photographer: John O'Hagan
page 49 (bottom):
Owners: James and Maureen Shotts, Tuscaloosa, Alabama
Designer: Ashley Garrison, Tuscaloosa, Alabama
Photographer: Cheryl Sales
page 50:
Owners: William and Becky Ketcher, Little Rock, Arkansas
Architect: Rick Redden, AIA, Little Rock, Arkansas
Photographer: John O'Hagan
page 51:
Architects: Robert Hammond, AIA, and Jay Huyett, AIA, Annapolis, Maryland
Photographer: John O'Hagan

Chapter 3 – ROOMS FOR COMPANY
page 52:
Architect: Gibson Worsham, Christiansburg, Virginia
Photographer: John O'Hagan
page 54:
Owners: Johnny and Johanna Aiken, Greenville, South Carolina
Architect: Robin Prince, AIA, Greenville, South Carolina
Designer: James Clamp, ASID, Greenville, South Carolina
Photographer: Cheryl Sales
page 55:
Owners: Jim and Dee McElroy, Atlanta, Georgia
Designer: Mary Cason, Columbia, South Carolina
Photographer: John O'Hagan
page 56:
Owners: James and Imelda Stevenson, Morgantown, West Virginia
Designer: Pat Bibbee, Charleston, West Virginia

Photographer: John O'Hagan
page 58:
Owners: Jon and Judy Zeder, Miami, Florida
Architect: Charles Harrison Pawley, AIA, Miami, Florida
Designers: Judi Male and Anita Margolis, Miami, Florida
Photographer: John O'Hagan
page 59:
Owners: Raymond and Frances Stewart, Greenville, South Carolina
Designer: James Clamp, ASID, Greenville, South Carolina
Photographer: Cheryl Sales
page 60:
Owners: Michael and Martita Vaughn, Lorena, Texas
Designer: William P. Davis, FASID, Waco, Texas
Photographer: Ardon Armstrong
page 61:
Owners: John and Kay Collett, Montgomery, Alabama
Architect: Frank Litchfield, AIA, Montgomery, Alabama
Designers: Jean Anderson and Judy Kyzer, Montgomery, Alabama
Photographer: Louis Joyner
page 62:
Owners: Robert and Susanne Adams, Alexandria, Virginia
Architect: Robert Bentley Adams, AIA, Alexandria, Virginia
Photographer: John O'Hagan
page 62 (inset):
Owners: Robert and Susanne Adams, Alexandria, Virginia
Architect: Robert Bentley Adams, AIA, Alexandria, Virginia
Photographer: John O'Hagan
page 63:
Owner: H. Joe Selby, Dallas, Texas
Designer: Deborah Forrest, ASID, Dallas, Texas
page 64:
Owners: John and Mary Allison, Little Rock, Arkansas
Architect: John Allison, AIA, Little Rock, Arkansas
Photographer: John O'Hagan
page 64 (inset):
Owners: John and Mary Allison, Little Rock, Arkansas
Architect: John Allison, AIA, Little Rock, Arkansas
Photographer: John O'Hagan
page 65 (top):
Owners: Mike and Genny Doramus, Dallas, Texas
Builder: Bob Forrest, Dallas, Texas

Photographer: John O'Hagan
page 65 (bottom):
Owners: Ron and Jeanene Hulsey,
Dallas, Texas
Designer: Richard Trimble, Dallas,
Texas
Photographer: John O'Hagan
page 66:
Owners: David and Leslie Cox,
Jackson, Mississippi
Architect: Ken Tate, Jackson, Missis-
sippi
Designer: Charme Tate, ASID,
Jackson, Mississippi
Photographer: John O'Hagan
page 67:
Owners: Ronald Kepes and Marilyn
Lazarus, South Miami, Florida
Designer: Marilyn Lazarus, South
Miami, Florida
Photographer: Cheryl Sales
page 68 (top):
Owners: D. Stephen and Diane
Walker, Charleston, West Virginia
Designer: Pat Bibbee, Charleston,
West Virginia
Photographer: Cheryl Sales
page 68 (bottom):
Owners: Rick and Laura Redden,
Little Rock, Arkansas
Architect: Rick Redden, AIA, Little
Rock, Arkansas
Photographer: John O'Hagan
page 69:
Owner/Designer: Michele Babcock,
Memphis, Tennessee
Photographer: Louis Joyner
page 70 (left):
Architect: Gibson Worsham, Chris-
tiansburg, Virginia
Photographer: John O'Hagan
page 70 (right):
Owners: Robert and Susanne Adams,
Alexandria, Virginia
Architect: Robert Bentley Adams,
AIA, Alexandria, Virginia
Photographer: John O'Hagan
page 71 (top):
Owners: John and Marilyn Cowles,
Arlington, Virginia
Designers: Gayle Smoker
Yoxtheimer, Alexandria, Virginia,
and Christine C. Benn, ASID, Arling-
ton, Virginia
Photographer: John O'Hagan
page 71 (bottom):
Owners: Mike and Carole Rose,
Nashville, Tennessee
Designer: Mark Simmons of Wm. M.
Hamilton and Associates, Nashville,
Tennessee

Photographer: Louis Joyner
page 72 (top):
Architect: Frank Welch, FAIA, Dallas,
Texas
Designer: Sydnie Wood, ASID,
Odessa, Texas
Photographer: Ardon Armstrong
page 72 (bottom):
Owners: Michael and Martita
Vaughn, Lorena, Texas
Designer: William P. Davis, FASID,
Waco, Texas
Photographer: Ardon Armstrong
page 73 (top left):
Owners: Louis and Gaye Joyner,
Birmingham, Alabama
Designer: Richard Tubb, Birming-
ham, Alabama
Photographer: Louis Joyner
page 73 (bottom left):
Owners: Phil and Sarah Nelson,
Jackson, Mississippi
Designer: Sarah Nelson, Jackson,
Mississippi
Photographer: John O'Hagan
page 74 (top):
Owners: James and Cathy Harvey,
Birmingham, Alabama
Designer: Tim Hargrove, Oxford,
Mississippi
Photographer: John O'Hagan
page 74 (bottom):
Owners: Rob and Anne Couch,
Birmingham, Alabama
Photographer: Cheryl Sales
page 75:
Owner: Glenda Tanner, Baton
Rouge, Louisiana
Designer: Helaine Moyse of Dixon
Smith Interiors, Baton Rouge, Lou-
isiana
Photographer: Cheryl Sales
page 76 (left):
Owners: Rick and Laura Redden,
Little Rock, Arkansas
Architect: Rick Redden, AIA, Little
Rock, Arkansas
Photographer: John O'Hagan
page 77:
Photographer: Cheryl Sales
page 78:
Owners: David and Leslie Cox,
Jackson, Mississippi
Architect: Ken Tate, Jackson, Missis-
sippi
Designer: Charme Tate, ASID,
Jackson, Mississippi
Photographer: John O'Hagan
page 79:
Architect: Gibson Worsham, Chris-
tiansburg, Virginia

Photographer: John O'Hagan
page 80:
Architects: Barbara Ball and Maynard
Ball, Alexandria, Virginia
Photographer: John O'Hagan
page 81:
Owners: Jim and Dee McElroy,
Atlanta, Georgia
Designer: Mary Cason, Columbia,
South Carolina
Photographer: John O'Hagan
page 82:
Owner: Glenda Tanner, Baton
Rouge, Louisiana
Designer: Helaine Moyse of Dixon
Smith Interiors, Baton Rouge, Lou-
isiana
Photographer: Cheryl Sales
page 83 (top):
Photographer: John O'Hagan
page 83 (bottom):
Owners: John and Carolyn Hartman,
Birmingham, Alabama
Photographer: John O'Hagan
page 84 (top):
Owners: James and Shara Overstreet,
Augusta, Georgia
Designer: Shara Overstreet, ASID,
Augusta, Georgia
Photographer: Cheryl Sales
page 84 (bottom left):
Owners: Roddy and Gail White,
Atlanta, Georgia
Designer: Liza Bryan, Atlanta,
Georgia
Photographer: Cheryl Sales
page 85 (top):
Owner: Carole Engle, Birmingham,
Alabama
Photographer: Cheryl Sales
page 85 (bottom right):
Owners: John and Mary Allison,
Little Rock, Arkansas
Architect: John Allison, AIA, Little
Rock, Arkansas
Photographer: Ardon Armstrong

Chapter 4 – **GRACIOUS DINING**

page 86:
Owners: Bob and Denise Pugh,
Germantown, Tennessee
Designer: Michele Babcock, Mem-
phis, Tennessee
Artist: David Mah, Memphis, Tennes-
see
Photographer: Louis Joyner
page 88:
Owner: Sandra Jacques, Nashville,
Tennessee
Designer: Deborah Tallent of
Wm. M. Hamilton and Associates,

Nashville, Tennessee
Photographer: Louis Joyner
page 90:
Owners: Scott and Cameron Vowell,
Birmingham, Alabama
Photographer: John O'Hagan
page 91:
Owners: John and Mary Allison,
Little Rock, Arkansas
Architect: John Allison, AIA, Little
Rock, Arkansas
Photographer: Louis Joyner
page 92:
Owners: Tom and Angela Rice,
Lexington, Kentucky
Designer: Barbara Ricks, ASID,
Lexington, Kentucky
Photographer: Bob Lancaster
page 93:
Owners: Mark and Fran Varel,
Dallas, Texas
Designer: Kathy Adcock-Smith,
ASID, Dallas, Texas
Photographer: Ardon Armstrong
page 94 (top):
Owners: Wade and Sissy Brodie,
Aiken, South Carolina
Designer: Julie Adams, Aiken, South
Carolina
Photographer: Cheryl Sales
page 94 (bottom):
Designer: Bitsy Duggins, Metairie,
Louisiana
Photographer: Cheryl Sales
page 95:
Owners: Randy and Liza Bryan,
Atlanta, Georgia
Architect: Norman Askins, Atlanta,
Georgia
Designer: Liza Bryan, Atlanta,
Georgia
Photographer: John O'Hagan
page 96:
Owners: James and Cathy Harvey,
Birmingham, Alabama
Designer: Tim Hargrove, Oxford,
Mississippi
Photographer: John O'Hagan
page 98 (left):
Owners: James and Maureen Shotts,
Tuscaloosa, Alabama
Designer: Ashley Garrison, Tus-
caloosa, Alabama
Photographer: John O'Hagan
page 98 (right):
Owners: Bill and Nancy Grogan,
Madison County, Mississippi
Photographer: John O'Hagan
page 99 (left):
Owners: James and Shara Overstreet,
Augusta, Georgia

Designer: Shara Overstreet, ASID,
Augusta, Georgia
Photographer: Cheryl Sales
page 99 (right):
Owners: Charlie and Beezie Towers,
Jacksonville, Florida
Photographer: John O'Hagan
page 100 (top):
Owners: Johnny and Johanna Aiken,
Greenville, South Carolina
Architect: Robin Prince, AIA, Green-
ville, South Carolina
Designer: James Clamp, ASID,
Greenville, South Carolina
Photographer: Cheryl Sales
page 100 (bottom):
Owner/Designer: Susan Swanson,
Tulsa, Oklahoma
Photographer: John O'Hagan
page 101 (top):
Owners: Edward and Abbie Voelker,
Alexandria, Louisiana
Architect: Gene Glankler, AIA,
Alexandria, Louisiana
Photographer: Bob Lancaster
page 101 (bottom):
Owner: Sandra Jacques, Nashville,
Tennessee
Designer: Deborah Tallent of Wm.
M. Hamilton and Associates, Nash-
ville, Tennessee
Photographer: Louis Joyner
page 102 (top right):
Owner/Designer: Charles Faudree,
Tulsa, Oklahoma
Architect: John Brooks Walton,
Tulsa, Oklahoma
Photographer: John O'Hagan
page 102 (center left):
Owners: Sam and Vicki
Batholomew, Nashville, Tennessee
Designer: Mark Simmons of Wm. M.
Hamilton and Associates, Nashville,
Tennessee
Photographer: Louis Joyner
page 102 (bottom right):
Designer: Charleane Borges Sample,
Birmingham, Alabama
Photographer: John O'Hagan
page 103 (top left):
Owners: Jim and Carol Dowdy,
Birmingham, Alabama
Photographer: John O'Hagan
page 103 (bottom left):
Owner/Designer: Cathy Harris,
Memphis, Tennessee
Photographer: John O'Hagan

Chapter 5 – SUNNY SPOTS

page 105:
Owners: Bill and Nancy Curtis,

Tampa, Florida
Designer: Marty Sears, Tampa,
Florida
Photographer: Cheryl Sales
page 106:
Owners: Bill and Nancy Curtis,
Tampa, Florida
Designer: Marty Sears, Tampa,
Florida
Photographer: Cheryl Sales
page 108:
Owners: Jack and Glenda Floyd,
Atlanta, Georgia
Designer: Jackye Lanham, Atlanta,
Georgia
Photographer: Louis Joyner
page 109:
Owners: Mitch and Olivia Mitchner,
Mount Vernon, Virginia
Architects: Calvert Bowie, AIA, and
Bill Gridley, AIA, Washington, D. C.
Photographer: John O'Hagan
page 110:
Owners: Peter and Gladys Stifel,
Kensington, Maryland
Architects: Heather Cass, AIA, and
Patrick Pinnell, AIA, Washington, D. C.
Photographer: John O'Hagan
page 112:
Owners: Dan and Judy Adcock,
Greenville, South Carolina
Designer: James Clamp, ASID,
Greenville, South Carolina
Photographer: Cheryl Sales
page 113:
Owners: J. C. and Phyllis Billingsley,
Little Rock, Arkansas
Designer: Phyllis Billingsley, ASID,
Little Rock, Arkansas
Photographer: Louis Joyner
page 114:
Owners: Jerry and Marsha Shive,
Greenville, South Carolina
Designer: Thea Furman Duffies,
Greenville, South Carolina
Photographer: Cheryl Sales
page 115 (bottom):
Owners: Bill and Nancy Curtis,
Tampa, Florida
Designer: Marty Sears, Tampa,
Florida
Photographer: Cheryl Sales

Chapter 6 – JUST FOR THE FAMILY

page 117:
Owner/Designer: Charles Faudree,
Tulsa, Oklahoma
Architect: John Brooks Walton, Tulsa,
Oklahoma
Photographer: John O'Hagan

page 150:
Owners: Burt and Cheryl Jarvis, Richmond, Virginia
Architect: Aquino and Winthrop Architects, Richmond, Virginia
Photographer: Cheryl Sales
page 151:
Owners: Steve and Kay Horrell, Nashville, Tennessee
Designer: Mark Simmons of Wm. M. Hamilton & Associates, Nashville, Tennessee
Photographer: Louis Joyner
page 152:
Owners: Jerry and Marsha Shive, Greenville, South Carolina
Designer: Thea Furman Duffies, Greenville, South Carolina
Photographer: Cheryl Sales
page 153 (top):
Owners: Greg and Carol Patton, Montgomery, Alabama
Architect: Robert McAlpine, AIA, Montgomery, Alabama
Photographer: John O'Hagan
page 153 (bottom):
Owners: William and Becky Ketcher, Little Rock, Arkansas
Architect: Rick Redden, AIA, Little Rock, Arkansas
Photographer: John O'Hagan
page 154:
Owners: Duane and Wendy Albrecht, Austin, Texas
Architect: David Hoffman, AIA, Austin, Texas
Photographer: Louis Joyner
page 155:
Owner: Elouise Cooper, Houston, Texas
Designer: Gay Fly, ASID, Houston, Texas
Photographer: Louis Joyner
page 156:
Owners: Henry and Julie Nathan, Waynesville, North Carolina
Architect: Dail Dixon, AIA, Chapel Hill, North Carolina
Photographer: Cheryl Sales
page 157:
Owners: George and Bess Miller, Tuscaloosa, Alabama
Architect: James H. Fitts III, AIA, Tuscaloosa, Alabama
Photographer: Cheryl Sales
page 158:
Owners: Mark and Jean Anderson, Montgomery, Alabama
Architect: Arthur Joe Grant, AIA, Montgomery, Alabama
Designer: Jean Anderson, Designers

Two, Montgomery, Alabama
Photographer: John O'Hagan
page 160:
Owners: Bill and Georgia Fae Leverett, Thomson, Georgia
Designer: Erman Fortenberry, Jr., ASID, of AGF, Inc., Atlanta, Georgia
Designer: Anne S. Brown, ASID, Augusta, Georgia
Kitchen designer: George Potter of Reliable Supply Co., Atlanta, Georgia
Photographer: John O'Hagan
page 161:
Owners: David and Leslie Cox, Jackson, Mississippi
Architect: Ken Tate, Jackson, Mississippi
Designer: Charme Tate, ASID, Jackson, Mississippi
Photographer: John O'Hagan
page 162:
Architect: Joe Stubblefield, AIA, San Antonio, Texas
Photographer: Ardon Armstrong
page 163:
Owners: Stephen and Dee Moses, New Orleans, Louisiana
Architect: A. G. Lyons, AIA, New Orleans, Louisiana
Photographer: John O'Hagan
page 164 (left):
Owners: Milton and Joan Schaeffer, Germantown, Tennessee
Designer: Dick Howell, Memphis, Tennessee
Photographer: Louis Joyner
page 165:
Owners: John and Leitha Barber, Galveston, Texas
Architect: Leslie Barry Davidson, AIA, Houston, Texas
Photographer: Ardon Armstrong
page 166 (left):
Owners: John and Barbara Wheeler, Charlotte, North Carolina
Architect: Hal Tribble, AIA, Charlotte, North Carolina
Photographer: John O'Hagan
page 166 (right):
Owner: Elouise Cooper, Houston, Texas
Designer: Gay Fly, ASID, Houston, Texas
Photographer: Louis Joyner
page 167 (top right):
Owners: Vincent and Mary Ann Bruno, Birmingham, Alabama
Designer: Kitchen Gallery, Birmingham, Alabama
Photographer: Bob Lancaster
page 167 (bottom left):

Owners: Duane and Wendy Albrecht, Austin, Texas
Architect: David Hoffman, AIA, Austin, Texas
Photographer: Louis Joyner
page 168 (top):
Owners: Jon and Michele Quistgaard=Petersen, Shreveport, Louisiana
Photographer: Mac Jamieson
page 168 (bottom):
Owners: John and Mary Allison, Little Rock, Arkansas
Architect: John Allison, AIA, Little Rock, Arkansas
Photographer: Louis Joyner
page 169 (top):
Owners: Henny and Jean Younes, Brownsboro, Alabama
Designer: LaMerle Mikell, Huntsville, Alabama
Photographer: Cheryl Sales
page 169 (bottom):
Owners: Steve and Reni Wenger, Asheville, North Carolina
Architect: James Samsel, AIA, Asheville, North Carolina
Photographer: Cheryl Sales
page 173:
Owners: George and Marilyn Sue Burgess III, Baton Rouge, Louisiana
Architect: A. Hays Town, AIA, Baton Rouge, Louisiana
Designer: Jo Emment, ASID, Baton Rouge, Louisiana
Photographer: John O'Hagan
page 174:
Owners: Jack and Emily Burwell, Huntsville, Alabama
Designer: Lynn DeYoung, ASID, Huntsville, Alabama
Photographer: Cheryl Sales
page 176 (bottom):
Architect: David Lake, AIA, San Antonio, Texas
Photographer: Ardon Armstrong
page 177 (top):
Owners: Bill and Nancy Curtis, Tampa, Florida
Designer: Marty Sears, Tampa, Florida
Photographer: Cheryl Sales
page 177 (bottom):
Photographer: Cheryl Sales
page 178:
Owners: Roger and Pat McGuire, Asheville, North Carolina
Architect: James Samsel, AIA, Asheville, North Carolina
Photographer: Cheryl Sales
page 179 (left):

Photographer: Ardon Armstrong
page 179 (right):
 Owners: Steve and Kay Horrell,
Nashville, Tennessee
Designer: Mark Simmons of Wm. M.
Hamilton & Associates, Nashville,
Tennessee
Photographer: Louis Joyner
page 180 (left):
 Owners: Robert and Carolyn Reed,
Mountain Brook, Alabama
Designer: Gary Snipes, Birmingham,
Alabama
Photographer: John O'Hagan
page 180 (top right):
 Owners: Robert and Carolyn Reed,
Mountain Brook, Alabama
Designer: Gary Snipes, Birmingham,
Alabama
Photographer: John O'Hagan
page 180 (bottom right):
 Owner: Glenda Tanner, Baton
Rouge, Louisiana
Designer: Helaine Moyse of Dixon
Smith Interiors, Baton Rouge, Louisi-
ana
Photographer: Cheryl Sales
page 181 (top left):
 Owners: David and Leslie Cox,
Jackson, Mississippi
Architect: Ken Tate, Jackson, Missis-
sippi
Designer: Charme Tate, ASID,
Jackson, Mississippi
Photographer: John O'Hagan
page 181 (right):
 Owners: John and Louise Slater,
Memphis, Tennessee
Designer: Michele Babcock, Mem-
phis, Tennessee
Photographer: Louis Joyner
page 181 (bottom left):
 Owner/Designer: Jim Pfaffman, AIA,
Birmingham, Alabama
Photographer: Cheryl Sales

Chapter 8 – **PERSONAL RETREATS**
page 182:
 Owners: Ron and Kay Hendricks,
Big Canoe, Georgia
Designer: Kay Hendricks of A Little
Bit of Everything, Atlanta, Georgia
Photographer: Cheryl Sales
page 185:
1988 Dallas Symphony Showhouse,
Dallas, Texas
Designer: Marguerite Theresa Green,
ASID, Dallas, Texas
Photographer: Hal Lott
page 186:
 Owners: John and Mary Allison,

Little Rock, Arkansas
Architect: John Allison, AIA, Little
Rock, Arkansas
Photographer: Louis Joyner
page 187:
1988 Dallas Symphony Showhouse,
Dallas, Texas
Designer: Stephen Dunn of Stephen
Dunn Designs, Dallas, Texas
Photographer: Hal Lott
page 188:
 Owners: Bob and Fran Murphy,
Greensboro, North Carolina
Designer: Fran Murphy, Greensboro,
North Carolina
Photographer: John O'Hagan
page 190:
Photographer: Cheryl Sales
page 191 (top):
 Owners: Ronald Kepes and Marilyn
Lazarus, South Miami, Florida
Designer: Marilyn Lazarus, South
Miami, Florida
Photographer: Cheryl Sales
page 191 (bottom):
 Owners: Roger and Pat McGuire,
Asheville, North Carolina
Architect: James Samsel, AIA,
Asheville, North Carolina
Photographer: Cheryl Sales
page 193:
 Designer: Leslie Fossler, ASID/IBD,
Austin, Texas
Photographer: Cheryl Sales
page 194:
 Owners: Fred and Becky Donatelli,
Alexandria, Virginia
Architect: John Cole, AIA, Alexan-
dria, Virginia
Photographer: John O'Hagan
page 195:
Photographer: John O'Hagan
page 196:
 Owners: Don and Beverly Campbell,
Dallas, Texas
Designer: Bob Forrest, Dallas, Texas
Photographer: John O'Hagan
page 197:
 Owner: Katherine Kinney, Asheville,
North Carolina
Architect: Robert Griffin, AIA,
Asheville, North Carolina
Photographer: Cheryl Sales
page 198:
 Owners: Allyn and Katherine
Thames, Montgomery, Alabama
Architect: James Barganier, AIA,
Montgomery, Alabama
Photographer: John O'Hagan
page 199 (top):
 Designer: Julie Wyatt, ASID,

Oklahoma City, Oklahoma
Photographer: John O'Hagan
page 199 (bottom):
 Owners: Butch and Julia West,
Columbia, Tennessee
Designer: Tom McCamp of L. Neal
Interiors, Nashville, Tennessee
Photographer: Louis Joyner
page 200:
Photographer: Cheryl Sales
page 202:
 Owners: John and Marilyn Cowles,
Arlington, Virginia
Designers: Gayle Smoker
Yoxtheimer, Alexandria, Virginia,
and Christine C. Benn, ASID, Arling-
ton, Virginia
Photographer: John O'Hagan
page 203:
 Owners: Larry and Linda Messina,
Baton Rouge, Louisiana
Designer: Helaine Moyse of Dixon
Smith Interiors, Baton Rouge, Lou-
isiana
Photographer: Cheryl Sales
page 204:
The National Symphony Decorators'
Show House, Washington, D. C.,
1988
Designers: Mary Beth McKeever
Confal and Joel Lilly Johnson of
Laura Ashley, Inc., Washington, D. C.
Photographer: Cheryl Sales
page 205:
1988 Dallas Symphony Showhouse,
Dallas, Texas
Designer: Ann Fox of Room Service
by Ann Fox, Dallas, Texas
Photographer: Hal Lott
page 206:
 Owners: Bill and Beth Lynn, Aiken,
South Carolina
Designer: Julie Adams, Aiken, South
Carolina
Photographer: Cheryl Sales
page 207:
 Owners: Stan and Judy Moser,
Waco, Texas
Designers: Jon McLean, ASID, and
Sandie McLean, ASID, Dallas, Texas
Photographer: Ardon Armstrong

214

GLOSSARY

A

accessories — small objects such as vases, plants, lamps, books, and decorative pieces

Adam Style — an eighteenth-century architectural and decorative style that used classical motifs, such as urns, swags, and wreaths

alcove — a recess or niche, usually large enough to contain seating, opening off of a larger room

andirons — the pair of metal supports for a fireplace log; also called firedogs

antique — a work of art, piece of furniture, or decorative object made before 1840; carpets made before 1700

antique finish — a paint or stain finish applied to an object and then wiped away to give an aged appearance

applied molding — molding applied to the surface of a wall or piece of furniture to give the effect of paneling

appliqué — decoration cut to shape and then fastened to a surface

apron — the horizontal structural member just below the top of a table, or below the seat of a chair

arch — a curved opening

area rug — a floor covering that covers only part of the floor

armoire — a large wardrobe or cupboard

art nouveau — a late nineteenth-century decorative style that featured stylized plant forms and elaborately curved decorative detail

Arts and Crafts Movement — a late nineteenth-century British art movement that stressed simple, handmade pieces

aubergine — an eggplant color

Aubusson — a type of tapestry-weave carpet

Austrian shade — a fabric window treatment that pulls up like a Roman shade, but with soft, billowing folds

Axminster — a tightly woven, cut pile carpet, whose pile is inserted in tufts into the weave

B

bachelor chest — a type of chest of drawers

bail handle — a drawer pull with a curved metal handle that hangs downward

baize — a felt-like woolen fabric often used to cover card tables

ball foot — a spherical wooden foot used for furniture legs

balloon shade — a window treatment with shirred or gathered fabric that pulls up into soft, billowy folds

baluster — the vertical support for a stair rail

balustrade — a stair rail atop a row of balusters

banding — an inlaid strip on furniture

banquette — an upholstered bench, often built-in

baroque — a seventeenth-century style of artistic expression marked by extravagant forms and elaborate ornamentation

barrel chair — a chair with curving sides and back

baseboard — the molding used along the bottom of a wall where it meets the floor

bas-relief — a type of sculpture where the design is only slightly raised above the background

batik — a method of wax resist dyeing for fabrics

Bauhaus — an influential German art school (1919-1932) that stressed the blending of design and mass production

bay window — a window or series of windows that form a recess in a room and project outward from the wall

beam — a horizontal framing member that supports a ceiling

bearing wall — a supporting, structural wall in a house

bench — a wide, backless seat

bentwood — furniture made from steam-bent strips of wood; a process developed in Austria-Hungary by nineteenth-century furniture maker Michael Thonet

Berber — an undyed, hand-knotted wool rug

Biedermeier — an early nineteenth-century German decorative style, with simple lines and often with painted-on details

bleaching — the chemical removal of color from fabric or wood

blockfront — a type of chest or highboy with raised panels on the front

bolection molding — molding used to frame wall panels

bolster — a cylindrical cushion

bombé — a curved front, as on a chest or commode

bonnet top — the broken-arch top of a secretary or highboy

book-match veneer — veneer with the grains matched so that one sheet of veneer appears to be the mirror image of the other

bowfront — an outward curving front, such as that of a chest

bow window — a window that curves outward, usually projecting less than a bay window

box pleat — a tailored fabric fold formed by two folded edges, one facing right and the other facing left

bracket — a right-angled support or reinforcement

brasses — decorative hardware made of brass

breakfront — a bookcase or cabinet whose center section projects forward

broadcloth — a tightly woven cloth, usually of cotton, with a smooth, lustrous finish

brocade — a heavy fabric with a raised, woven design

broken pediment — a triangular gable with a section removed at the top, usually used above the cornice of cabinets, mirrors, grandfather clocks, and similar furniture; the space is often filled with a decorative urn

bronze-doré — gilded bronze

buckram — a coarse fabric, heavily sized, used to stiffen draperies

buffet — a sideboard

bullnose edge — a half-round molding or edging

bun foot — a flattened variation of the ball foot; often found on Flemish furniture

bureau — a writing desk; a low chest of drawers

burl — an outgrowth on a tree, often used for veneer

burlap — a coarse, loosely woven jute or hemp cloth

butler's tray table — a small table with hinged sides and ends that fold up to form a tray

C

cabinet — a case or cupboard, either freestanding or built-in

cabriole leg — a curved furniture leg that resembles a stylized animal leg tapering to an ornamental foot; characteristically found on Queen Anne, Georgian, and Louis XV furniture

cachepot — an ornamental container for a flowerpot

cafe curtains — short curtains hung on a rod

camelback — a chair with a curved top rail

camelback sofa — a type of sofa with a curved (humped) back, typically seen in Queen Anne, Chippendale, and Federal styles

campaign chest — a portable chest of drawers used by military officers in the field

candelabra — a branched, ornamental candlestick

canopy bed — a bed with a fabric cover supported by four posts

canvas — a heavy, closely woven cloth, usually of cotton, flax, or hemp

capital — the decorative top of a column

captain's bed — a single platform bed with built-in drawers below

captain's chair — a wooden, spindle-back armchair

carcase — the basic wooden framework of a piece of case goods

carpet — a woven floor covering, usually used to refer to a wall-to-wall carpet as opposed to rug, which refers to a floor covering that covers only one area of the floor

carved rug — a rug with the pile cut to create a three-dimensional design

case goods — furniture designed for storage, such as dressers, cabinets, desks, and bookcases

casement window — a window that is hinged along one side and opens by swinging out; often used in pairs

cathedral ceiling — a high, sloping ceiling

chair rail — a piece of molding placed about thirty inches above the floor to protect the wall from being marred by chair backs

chaise longue — a chair long enough for reclining

chamfer — a beveled edge

chandelier — a hanging, often ornate, light fixture

chest of drawers — a piece of furniture containing a set of drawers, primarily used to store clothing

chest-on-chest — a double chest of drawers, with one stacked atop the other

Chesterfield — a large, overstuffed sofa with arms and back of the same height

chiffonier — a high, narrow chest of drawers; also a nineteenth-century English term for a sideboard with doors

chimney breast — the projecting section of wall above and on each side of a fireplace

Chinese Chippendale — the Chinese-influenced work of eighteenth-century English cabinetmaker Thomas Chippendale; the Chinese influence is evident in trellis designs, pagodas, and Oriental figures

chinoiserie — Chinese-inspired decoration popular in eighteenth-century England and France

Chippendale, Thomas (1718-1779) — influential English cabinetmaker and furniture designer

chroma — the intensity or brilliance of a color

claw-and-ball foot — a furniture foot carved in the shape of a stylized bird or animal claw holding a ball

clerestory — an outside wall, with windows, rising above an adjoining roof

cloisonné — a type of enamel decoration in which the design is formed by enameled areas outlined with narrow strips of metal

club chair — a low, upholstered easy chair

coffee table — a low table used in front of a sofa

colonnade — a row of columns

column — a vertical support post

commode — a low chest of drawers or cabinet

console table — a long, narrow table set against the wall, often supported by wall-mounted brackets instead of legs

corduroy — a cotton fabric woven with vertical ridges

Corinthian order — the most ornate of the three Greek classical architectural orders, characterized by its bell-shaped capital surrounded with stylized acanthus leaves

corner cupboard — a triangular cupboard designed to fit into a corner of a room

cornice — the horizontal molding at the top of a wall or building

Coromandel screen — a Chinese lacquered folding screen decorated with low relief carvings

couch — a piece of furniture for sitting or reclining

country — sturdy, simplified furniture

credenza — a buffet or sideboard

crepe — a light fabric with a crinkled texture

crystal — a clear, colorless quartz glass

cupboard — a storage cabinet with doors

curtain — a fabric used to screen a window

cushion — a pillow

cut pile — fabric woven with a loop pile which is then cut; velvet is an example of a fabric with a cut pile

D

dado — the portion of the wall below the chair rail; also called wainscot

dado cap — the top piece of molding of the dado; also called a chair rail

damask — a lustrous fabric with flat patterns in a satin weave

davenport — a large upholstered sofa; also a small writing desk

daybed — a small, single bed used either as a bed or a lounge chair

delft — glazed earthenware with blue and white decoration, originally made in Delft, Netherlands

demilune — literally half-moon; French term for a semicircular window

den — an informal library or retreat; a family room

denier — a unit of fineness for silk or synthetic yarn; the smaller the number, the finer the yarn

denim — a coarse cloth, usually woven with a colored warp thread and a white woof thread

dentil — one of a series of toothlike blocks used in a row as decoration under a cornice

dhurrie — a flat-woven, reversible rug made in India; usually woven of wool or cotton

dimmer — a type of electrical switch that can regulate the intensity of a lighting unit

dinette — a small table with chairs used in the kitchen or breakfast room for informal meals

Directoire — the style of the French Directory of the mid-1790s occurring between the Louis XVI and Empire styles

distressed — furniture that has been scratched or worn through use; artificially simulated on some new pieces

divan — a couch or bench without back or arms

documentary prints — new wallpaper or fabric copied from period patterns

Doric order — the simplest and oldest of the classic Greek architectural orders

dotted swiss — a muslin fabric with an evenly spaced embossed dot design

double-hung window — a window with an upper sash that can be lowered, as well as a lower sash that can be raised

drape — a drapery for a window; the way a fabric hangs; to arrange a fabric in folds

drapery — a draped fabric window treatment

draw curtain or draw draperies — curtains or draperies mounted on a horizontal traverse rod so that they can be closed with a cord

drawing room — originally, a sitting room to which people withdrew after dinner; a formal reception room

draw table — a table whose top surface can be enlarged by pulling out end leaves

dresser — originally a sideboard or cabinet; a chest of drawers

dressing room — a room usually off of the bathroom and bedroom used for dressing

dressing table — a small table with a kneehole and often with drawers and a mirror

drill — a cotton or linen twillweave fabric

dropped ceiling — a false ceiling installed below an existing one, often used to hide exposed piping or ductwork

dry sink — a wooden cabinet with a basin, used before the advent of indoor plumbing

duck — a canvas-like cotton fabric

dust ruffle — a fabric skirt that extends from the bottom of the mattress to the floor, used to conceal the box springs and bed frame

Dutch foot — a foot of a cabriole leg suggesting a hoof

E

Early American — the style of art and architecture characteristic of colonial America; also, American Colonial

ears — molding pieces which extend outward beyond the side frames of doors or windows

easy chair — a comfortable upholstered chair

eclectic — a blending of pieces from several styles

egg and dart — a type of molding with stylized eggs and darts repeated alternately; also called egg and tongue or egg and anchor

embroidery — a fabric decorated with hand or machine needlework designs

Empire — an early nineteenth-century French decorative style characterized by classic and Egyptian motifs; also adapted by Thomas Sheraton in England and Duncan Phyfe in America

end table — a small table used at the end of a couch; usually about the height of the arm of a chair

enrichment — a carved, repetitive design on a molding

entablature — in classical architecture, the part of the structure resting on the columns; the entablature consists of the architrave, frieze, and cornice

epergne — an ornamental, tiered serving dish often used as a centerpiece

escutcheon — the decorative plate surrounding a keyhole

étagère — a piece of furniture with open shelves for displaying small objects

F

facade — the front face of a building

faconne — a fabric with a fancy weave, often with a pattern consisting of small scattered figures

fanlight — a semicircular transom window

fauteuil — French word for armchair

faux — French word for fake

faux bois — fake wood; usually a painted-on wood grain

Federal — the decorating style that was popular in America just after the American Revolution and into the 1830s; characterized by classical motifs

felt — a nonwoven cloth, usually of wool

fender — an iron or brass rail set on the hearth to protect the floor from sparks or embers

fenestration — the arrangement of windows and doors on the facade of a building

festoon — a garland of leaves, flowers, or fruit; or a carved wood representation of a decorative chain or garland

fiddleback chair — a chair with a back splat shaped like a violin or vase

field — the flat background surface of a panel

filigree — a type of delicate ornamental work, usually made from fine, twisted wire

finial — the decorative ornament at the top of an object

fireback — a metal or cast-iron panel placed in the back of an open fireplace used to reflect heat into the room

firedogs — andirons

fire irons — fireplace tools such as poker, shovel, and tongs

fire screen — a protective, metal screen before a fireplace, used to keep sparks from escaping into the room; or a solid screen used to block the heat from the fire

flare — the outward spread of chair legs

flat — a type of paint finish with no gloss or sheen

flight — an uninterrupted series of steps between floors or between a floor and a landing

flock paper — a type of wallpaper with a velvety-surface pattern

floorcloth — a woven canvas cloth, usually with a painted surface, used as a rug

fluting — parallel decorative grooves in a column, pilaster, or piece of furniture

footrail — the horizontal stretcher between the front legs of a chair

four-poster — a bed with tall corner posts, which can be used to support a canopy

foyer — an entranceway

frame — the molding surrounding a painting or print; or the skeleton of an upholstered furniture piece

fretwork — ornamental openwork, often used for brackets, table galleries, and chair backs, as in the Chippendale style

G

gallery — a decorative border or railing around a tabletop or shelf; also, a porch

garderobe — a wardrobe or armoire

garland — a decorative wreath

gateleg table — a drop-leaf table with legs that swing out to support the leaves

gauze — a thin, transparent fabric

Georgian — the period in eighteenth-century and early nineteenth-century England relating to the reigns of the first four Georges; popular styles include Adam, Chippendale, Hepplewhite, and Sheraton

German silver — a metal alloy of copper, zinc, and nickel

gilding — a thin, decorative covering of gold or gold paint applied to furniture, picture frames, or other objects

gimp — an ornamental fabric braid, often used to cover seams or upholstery tacks

gingham — a cotton fabric with a checkered design

glaze — a gloss or shine; a clear liquid used in novelty paint finishes

glazing — the glass in windows or doors

grass cloth — a wall covering made from strips of coarse grass attached to a paper backing

Greek Revival — the classically influenced architectural style of the early nineteenth century

grosgrain — a close-woven fabric or ribbon with narrow ribs or cords

ground — the background color of a wall; the framing of a wall

grout — a mortar used to fill the spaces between tiles

gypsum board — a type of wall material consisting of gypsum sandwiched between paper; typical size is 4 x 8 feet and thickness is ½ inch

H

hall tree — a hat and coat rack

hardware — the metal handles, hinges, and pulls on furniture or cabinets

hardwood — wood from broad-leaved, deciduous trees such as oak, maple, walnut, and mahogany

hassock — a type of footstool

hearth — the flat, horizontal surface at the base and in front of the fireplace

Hepplewhite — a late eighteenth-century furniture style with delicate, curving lines and often featuring shield-back chairs

highboy — a tall chest of drawers on legs

Hollywood bed — a metal bed frame without a footboard; a headboard (often upholstered) may be attached to the frame or to the wall

hue — a color, such as red, yellow, blue, or green

hunt board — a type of sideboard with drawers

hutch — a cupboard with open shelves

I

indirect lighting — lighting which is reflected off of a surface

inglenook — a recessed area with seating beside a fireplace

inlay — a decorative pattern or design made by inserting wood, metal, or other material into a flat surface

intaglio — an engraving or decorative pattern carved into stone or other hard material

Ionic order — the classical order of architecture characterized by columns topped with a capital having scroll-like volutes

J

jabot — the cascading fabric at each side of a swagged valance

Jacquard — a fabric with an intricate weave or pattern

jalousie — a type of window with horizontal, unframed glass panels that pivot to open

jamb — the inside of a door frame

japan — a varnish that yields a hard, glossy finish

jardiniere — an ornamental plant stand

Jenny Lind bed — a wood bed made with decorative, spool-shaped turnings

jib door — a door which is designed to appear as part of the wall

joist — a horizontal structural member used to support a floor or ceiling

K

KD [knocked down] — furniture sold finished but unassembled

kerf — a cut made by a saw

kickplate — a metal plate used to protect the lower face of a door

knee — the upper part of a cabriole leg, often decorated with relief carving

knife box — a small chest or box used to hold knives

L

lacquer — a type of finish; can be either clear or colored

ladder-back — a chair with a back consisting of two upright posts connected by a series of horizontal slats which resemble the rungs of a ladder

lambrequin — a decorative board, often fabric covered, mounted at the top of a window to cover the drapery rod; also, a short decorative drapery for a shelf edge or window

landing — a platform on a stair between floors

lath — a thin strip of wood used as a support for plaster or stucco

lattice — an open screen made of wood lath

lauan — a hardwood from the Philippines that resembles true mahogany

lavabo — a spigot and washbasin that are fastened to a wall; often used for decoration as a planter

Lawson sofa — a type of sofa with simple, squared-off lines and high square or rolled arms

lining paper — a special wallpaper that is used as a base for the decorative paper; the lining paper is often used to cover cracks and other irregularities in the wall

lintel — a horizontal structural member over a door or window

load-bearing wall — a wall that supports the ceiling or roof

loggia — a roofed arcade, gallery, or colonnade open along one side

Louis XIV — French decorative style during the reign of Louis XIV (1643-1715) characterized by ornate, rich baroque style of furnishings

Louis XV — French decorative style during the reign of Louis XV (1715-1774) characterized by furniture with graceful curves; styles often revealed some Chinese influence

Louis XVI — French decorative style during the reign of Louis XVI (1774-1792) marked by a return to classical simplicity

lounge — a sofa or couch with one arm

love seat — a sofa designed for two people

lowboy — a low chest or side table

lunette — a semicircular window

M

mahogany — a type of tropical hardwood that was especially popular in the Georgian period

majolica — a type of earthenware, usually with a brightly colored glaze

mantel — the shelf above a fireplace

marbleizing — decorative painting of a surface to resemble marble

marquetry — decorative inlay work

mission — a style of furniture patterned after the furniture used in the early Spanish missions of the southwestern United States

modillion — an ornamental bracket

moiré — a type of fabric finish with a watered, wavy appearance

molding — decorative strips of wood used to conceal joints and give a more decorative, finished look

monk's cloth — a heavy, coarse cotton fabric; generally used for draperies

monochrome — a color scheme composed of tints and shades in a single hue

morris chair — an easy chair with adjustable back and removable cushions

mortar — the cement-based bonding material for masonry construction

mounts — cabinet hardware such as pulls, escutcheons, and handles

mullion — the vertical member that forms a division between units of a window

muntin — the horizontal and vertical strips that hold the individual panes of glass in a window

muslin — a sturdy, plain-weave cotton fabric, often unbleached

N

neoclassicism — an eighteenth-century stylistic movement based on Greek and Roman art and architecture; the English Adam style and French Louis XVI are examples of the neoclassic style

neutral — a color, such as white, black, gray, or tan, that blends well with other colors

niche — a recess in a wall often used to display sculpture

night table — a bedside table

nosing — the curved front edge of a stair tread

O

objet d'art — a small decorative object or accessory of some artistic value

occasional table — a small, multi-use table

ogee — a molding with adjoining concave and convex curves creating an S-shaped profile

organdy — a thin, transparent muslin with a stiff finish

ormolu — gilded brass or bronze used for ornamentation

ottoman — an overstuffed footstool

overdoor — a decorative panel, usually glazed, set over a doorway

P

pad foot — a simple, rounded furniture foot, as on Queen Anne cabriole legs

palette — the range of colors

Palladian window — a unit consisting of a central arched window flanked by two more narrow windows with square heads; named after Andrea Palladio (1508-1580), an Italian architect

pane — a single piece of glass in a window

parlor — a living room

parquet — a floor composed of many small blocks of wood arranged in a pattern

Parsons table — a rectangular table with straight legs that are flush with the tabletop; named after Parsons School of Design

pastel — a light, pale tint of a color

patina — the mellow, timeworn look of a surface

patio — a courtyard or outdoor dining or recreation area adjoining a house

pedestal — a supporting base for a table; a stand for a vase or sculpture

pediment — the triangular end of a gable; also, the triangular top for a doorway or cabinet

Pembroke table — a type of eighteenth-century table with two drop leaves and a drawer

percale — a closely woven cotton fabric

pergola — an arbor or garden structure

petit point — finely-stitched needlepoint

pewter — an alloy of tin and other metals, such as lead, antimony, or copper

piano nobile — the main floor of a house

pickling — a furniture finish created by painting a piece, then wiping away most of the paint before it has dried, leaving some paint in the cracks and corners

picture molding — a horizontal molding set near the ceiling and used to support artwork

piecrust table — a round table with a raised, decorative edge

piercework — openwork as in the splat of a Chippendale chair

pie safe — a cupboard with pierced-tin panels, used to store pies

pilaster — a rectangular engaged column that projects slightly outward from the adjoining wall

pile — the loops or tufts of a carpet that form the wear surface

pinwale — a narrow-ribbed corduroy

piping — a decorative fabric trimming used to edge pillows or upholstered furniture

piqué — a heavy, ribbed fabric

plinth — the square base block of a column or pilaster

plush — a fabric with a thick, deep pile

polychrome — many-colored

pongee — a raw silk fabric with nubby slubs, usually natural tan in color

porcelain — a hard, translucent type of ceramic ware

primary colors — three colors–red, yellow, and blue–from which all other colors may be derived

primitive — art or craft characterized by simple, often naive forms and unschooled technique

priscilla curtains — ruffled, pullback curtains with a short, ruffled valance, usually of a sheer fabric

proportion — the relationship of one part of an object to the other parts or to the whole

provincial — a decorative style characterized by simplicity and informality, with furnishings that are unsophisticated in design

puce — a dark red color

pull-up chair — a lightweight occasional chair that can be moved easily

Q

Queen Anne — English decorative style during the reign of Queen Anne (1702-1714) typified by furniture with curved backs and legs (the cabriole leg), and Chinese-inspired claw-and-ball feet and lacquer work

quion — the corner of a building, often articulated with stone or brick

quirk — a groove in a molding

R

rafters — the structural members that support the roof

rag rug — an area rug woven from fabric scraps

rail — a structural member or support

rake — the slope from vertical, as in a chair back

rattan — a part of the stem of a palm used to make casual furniture; the stems are bent to form the furniture frame

recess — a niche or alcove

reeding — a small convex molding, the reverse of fluting

Regency — the English decorative style during George IV's regency as Prince of Wales (1811-1820) characterized by the use of Chinese and Egyptian motifs

relief — carving or decoration that stands out from a surface

Renaissance — the European period beginning in the fourteenth century and lasting into the seventeenth century; marked by a revival of classical influence expressed in the arts, architecture, and sciences

ribband back — a chair back, as on some Chippendale-style chairs, carved to resemble an interlacing ribbon

rickrack — a flat braid in a zigzag pattern, used for trim

rise — the vertical dimension between two stair treads

riser — the vertical surface of a step between two treads

rococo — an excessively ornate artistic style of the eighteenth century characterized by fanciful curves and elaborate ornamentation; in France, this was the style of Louis XV; in England, the Chippendale style

Roman shade — a tailored, fabric window shade that hangs as a flat panel and is raised by cords to fold accordian-style

runner — a long, narrow area rug used in an entrance hall or on a stairway

rush — a type of marsh plant used to weave chair seats, often seen on American country pieces

rya rug — a Scandinavian shag rug

S

saber leg — an inward-curving chair leg copied from Grecian chairs and used on some Sheraton chairs

sanguine — a moderate to strong red color (from the French word for blood)

sash — the framework which holds the panes of glass in a window; in a double-hung window, one sash raises, the other lowers

sateen — a cotton fabric with lustrous face and dull back

satin — a fabric (usually silk) with a smooth, glossy face and a dull back

scale — the relationship of an object to another object; the relationship of an object to the human body (human scale); the relationship of the size of a drawing to the size of the actual object

sconce — a wall-mounted light fixture

screen — a freestanding panel that is used to hide or divide

scroll — a decorative carving that imitates the spiral of loosely coiled parchment or paper

scroll pediment — a broken pediment with symmetrically balanced arches ending in scroll-like spirals

secondary color — color produced by mixing two of the primary colors; orange, green, and violet are the secondary colors

secondary wood — the less expensive wood used for unexposed parts of furniture

Second Empire — the French decorative style (also called late Empire) developed under Napoleon III

(1852-1871) and characterized by heavy, ornate furnishings that combined Empire and Louis XV motifs

secretary — a fold-out writing desk with drawers below and bookcases above

sectional furniture — modular furniture that can be used separately or combined to make a larger unit

section drawing — a drawing that shows an object as if sliced in half

selvage — the reinforced woven edge of a piece of fabric finished as to prevent raveling

serigraph — a silk-screen color print

set — a matching grouping

settee — a high-backed upholstered bench, often designed to resemble a row of chairs

settle — a high-backed, usually wooden bench, often with a lift-up seat for storage

shade — a color with black added to darken or make it more gray

Shaker style — simple, unadorned furniture made in the eighteenth and nineteenth centuries by the Shaker religious sect

shantung — a heavy, rough-textured silk fabric

sheer — a lightweight, transparent fabric

Sheraton — Thomas Sheraton (1751-1806), English cabinetmaker; a style of furniture characterized by straight lines and graceful design

shirring — the gathering of fabric on a rod, as for curtains

sideboard — a piece of furniture used in the dining room and having compartments for serving pieces

side chair — an armless chair

side table — pedestals or commodes used at either end of a sideboard, usually designed to be placed against a wall

sill — the horizontal member at the base of a window

sisal — a fiber used to make floor mats and area rugs

skirt — the horizontal frame of a table just below the top; also, a fabric apron around the base of a table, chair, or bed that hides the legs

slat — a horizontal member in the back of a chair

sleigh bed — a type of bed with scrolled headboard and footboard that resembles a sleigh

slipcover — an easily removable fabric cover for a chair or couch

slipper chair — a low-seated upholstered chair without arms

slip seat — an upholstered chair seat that can be removed easily for cleaning or reupholstering

slub — an uneven section in a yarn which gives fabric a rough texture

socle — a plain square pedestal

sofa — a long, upholstered seat with arms and a back; a couch

sofa table — a long, rectangular table used behind a sofa

soffit — the underside of a structural member such as an arch or beam

solarium — a sunroom

spindle — a turned, rod-shaped, decorative piece

splat — the central upright member of the back of a chair

splay — angled outward, as in a chair leg

squab — a loose chair or couch cushion

sterling — a silver alloy having a fixed standard of purity

stile — the vertical framing members of a paneled wall; the vertical frame of a chest or other piece of case goods

stippling — a decorative painting technique done by dabbing paint onto a surface with a sponge, brush, or crumpled paper

stoneware — a heavy, opaque, nonporous ceramic ware

stool — a backless and armless seat or footrest

stretcher — a horizontal brace or support in a chair or table located between the apron and the floor, usually extending between two legs

strié — a solid-color fabric woven with a subtle stripe; also, wallpaper or painting with a subtle, striped design

stucco — a plaster or cement material used as a decorative finish on walls

stuck molding — molding formed in the surface of an object, rather than separately applied

stud — a vertical framing member in a wall, usually 2 x 4 lumber, spaced sixteen inches apart

studio couch — an upholstered, backless couch that may be converted into a double bed; a daybed

study — a room, usually with a desk, that is used as a library or home office

style — the decorative design of an object or room

swag — a fabric window treatment consisting of cloth loosely draped over a rod

swatch — a small sample of fabric

swiss — a crisp, sheer cotton cloth (see dotted swiss)

symmetrical — formal, mirror-image balance

T

tabby — a plain-woven fabric; moiré-finish silk fabric

taffeta — a smooth, lustrous fabric

tallboy — a double chest of drawers

tambour — a flexible, rolling top on a desk

tapestry — a heavy fabric with a woven design; often displayed as a wall hanging

tassel — a decorative fabric ornament used at the edge or corners of pillows or draperies

terrace — a paved outdoor area, often raised

terra-cotta — reddish brown fired clay used for flower pots, floor tiles, and garden ornaments

terrazzo — a mosaic floor consisting of concrete made with small pieces of marble or granite

tertiary color — color made by mixing two secondary colors

tester — a canopy on a bed

tete-à-tete — an S-shaped, two-person couch with seats facing in opposite directions

texture — the surface finish of an object, either actual or visual

thousand-legged table — a type of gateleg table

ticking — a sturdy cotton or linen fabric, usually striped, and often used as a covering for pillows

tieback — a decorative fabric, cord, or metal hook used to hold a drapery open

tilt-top table — an occasional table with a hinged top that can be tilted up for storage

toilet table — dressing table

tole — decorative objects, such as boxes, lamp shades, and trays, made of painted sheet metal

torchère — a floor lamp, usually directing the light upward

tortoiseshell — a decorative veneer made from the shell of a turtle; also, a painted finish resembling tortoiseshell

transitional — a style that combines elements from two different styles

transom — a window set over a door

trapunto — a raised, decorative, quilted design

travertine — a porous mineral formed by deposition from spring waters, usually cream in color

tray table — a serving tray supported by a stand

tread — the horizontal part of a stair

trestle — a heavy supporting beam, such as that used in a trestle table

tricot — type of cotton or synthetic fabric with a close inelastic knit

trim — the decorative molding in a room or on a piece of furniture; also, fabric ornamentation, especially at edges or seams

tripod — a three-legged table or stand

triptych — a three-paneled picture or carving

trivet — a small metal stand with short feet, for use under a hot dish on the table

trompe l'oeil — painting done on a flat surface to resemble a realistic, three-dimensional scene

trumeau — an overmantel or over-door panel

trumeau mirror — a framed mirror with a scene painted on a panel which is mounted over the mirror

trundle bed — a low bed that can be stored beneath a regular bed when not in use

tub chair — an easy chair with a rounded, barrel-shaped back

Tuscan order — one of the five classical orders of Roman architecture, marked by a simple style

tuxedo sofa — a simple sofa with arms the same height as the back

tweed — a fabric, usually wool, with a rough, nubby texture

twill — a twill weave fabric having the appearance of diagonal lines

tympanum — the triangular vertical surface of a pediment

U

uprights — the vertical frame pieces of a chair that form the back legs and continue up to form the sides of the back

V

valance — a decorative covering, either fabric or wood, used to hide the rod of a drapery or other window treatment

value — the lightness or darkness of a color

vase — a decorative container or urn

velour — a fabric with a napped surface resembling velvet

velvet — a fabric with a short, soft, dense pile

velveteen — a cotton velvet

veneer — a thin sheet of expensive or finely-grained wood glued to an inferior wood

venetian blind — a window treatment consisting of a series of horizontal slats that can be turned or raised to control light or privacy

veranda — a long, covered porch

verdigris — a greenish blue patina that forms on copper, brass, or bronze surfaces

vestibule — an entry or foyer

Victorian — the English decorative style during the reign of Queen Victoria (1837-1901) characterized by luxurious velvets and brocades, both on upholstered pieces and on walls

vitrine — a wall-mounted, glass-front china cabinet

W

wainscot — paneling; often used to refer to the lower part of an interior wall when finished differently from the remainder of the wall

wardrobe — a large chest or cupboard in which clothes may be hung

Welsh dresser — a sideboard with open shelves above and often with closed cupboards and drawers below; also called a Welsh cupboard

whatnot — a shelf unit designed to hold small decorative objects

wicker — small strips of fiber or wood woven into furniture or baskets

William and Mary — English decorative style during the reign of William and Mary (1689-1702) characterized by walnut furniture, grained veneers, trumpet legs, and needlepoint upholstery

Windsor chair — a wooden chair with a spindle back and usually a saddle seat

wine cooler — a small container used to keep wine cool during a meal

wing chair — an upholstered armchair with a high back and sides

worsted — a fabric woven from long wool fibers and having a firm, napless texture

INDEX

Italics indicate sketches